Managing Alone

Your Trusted Advisors' Guide to
Surviving the Death of Your Spouse

Jennifer Black, CFP
&
Janet Baccarani, CFP

Published and distributed by

Bacc 'N Black Corp.
714 Burnhamthorpe Rd. E.
Mississauga, ON   Canada   L4Y 2X3
Tel: 905-896-8373
Email: info@dedicatedfinancialsolutions.ca
www.createwealthnow.ca
www.widowed.ca

Although the authors have exhaustively researched all sources to ensure the accuracy and completeness of the information contained in this book, they assume no responsibility for errors, inaccuracies, omissions or inconsistencies herein. Any slights of people or organizations are unintentional. Readers should use their own judgment and/or consult financial and legal experts for specific applications to their individual situations.

Editor: Donna Dawson, CPE
Cover design: Mod Graphic
Photographer: LV Imagery
Page composition: Sheila Mahoney

ISBN 978-0-9920183-0-6
Printed in Canada.

"I met Jennifer at a very vulnerable time in my life. About seven months prior, my husband had died suddenly and I had been inundated with financial advisors trying to get me to work with them on the financial aspects of his estate. I was totally unprepared because he was the one who had managed the finances. I was also dealing with a disabled daughter who had started her path to semi-independent living. I questioned how I was going to not only plan for this, but how was I going to afford it?

When I met with Jennifer, I instantly felt at ease. Jennifer had asked me to bring in everything I felt would pertain to my financial situation and, I have to admit, I really wasn't sure what 'everything' was or meant so I took everything! Jennifer did not laugh or make me feel inadequate. She reassured me by looking at each document and reviewing what it was and meant. I left feeling so relieved. I was sure I had made the right decision in talking to Jennifer.

I recently met again with Jennifer. I am now aware of all my investments as well as my spending. Jennifer listened to me. I cannot emphasize enough how important that was to me. Anytime I have a question or I need to talk to anyone at Dedicated Financial Solutions, they have been there for me.

The personal, patient guidance that I was given at one of the most difficult times in my life will forever be remembered."

~Linda Broadbent, Widow

"I trust both Janet and Jennifer very much. They provide me with the peace of mind that my finances are in good health."

~Nely Laning, Widow

"Highly recommended! Doing a great job with my investments and I trust them. Janet and Jennifer are pleasant people to deal with and always keep me well informed about the activity in my portfolio."

~Arleen Wig, Widow

"The loss of a spouse triggers an emotional avalanche that is only made more devastating by the financial concerns that so often come crashing in at the same time. Much has been written about dealing with the 'feeling' side of the equation – not enough about the money side. *Managing Alone* fills that void – comprehensively and compassionately. Using real life stories and real life solutions, based on their extensive experience as financial advisors, Jennifer Black and Janet Baccarani offer insight, counsel, direction, encouragement and, most importantly, specific information to guide recent widows and widowers through the financial transition to the next stage of their lives. This book could be the most valuable gift anyone could give or receive."

~George Hartman, Managing Director, Accretive Advisor

"*Managing Alone* illustrates how you don't have to be alone when it comes to handling your finances after losing someone you care deeply about. This book uses anecdotal situations to explore options, is easy to comprehend and provides great advice."

~Pattie Lovett-Reid, Chief Financial Commentator, CTV News

To my parents who taught me values and encouraged me along the way. To my husband, Kevin, without whom I could not have done any of this. To my daughters, Sara and Kayla, who teach me something new each day and remind me to live.

~ Jennifer Black

Contents

About the Authors

Jennifer Black BSEd, CFP, FMA, CPCA, FCSI, CIM

After a successful tennis career, Jennifer joined Janet in the financial industry in 2003. Jennifer quickly discovered how much she enjoys working with people and helping them to achieve their goals. Leveraging the discipline and work ethic developed during her tennis career, Jennifer has been instrumental in creating the successful process used by Dedicated Financial Solutions. Each meeting has a specific focus, ensuring that clients are always accomplishing something that will move them closer to achieving their goals.

As a Certified Financial Planner and Canadian Investment Manager, Jennifer has an inherent ability to understand clients' needs, help them clarify their goals and develop portfolios to help them reach those goals quickly and efficiently. Jennifer is co-owner of Dedicated Financial Solutions and is also a financial advisor with a Canadian investment dealer where she currently has the honour of sitting on the Advisory Council.

Jennifer still enjoys playing tennis and also enjoys golf and spending time with family. She lives in Mississauga with her husband, Kevin, and their two daughters. She enjoys watching her daughters find their passions and work toward their own goals.

Janet Baccarani, BSc, MBA, CPA, CA, CFP, FMA, CPCA

As a Chartered Accountant and Certified Financial Planner, Janet has assisted clients with tax-related matters and in creating and preserving wealth for their families since 1998. She is dedicated to helping her clients find the right blend of wealth creation and preservation for their long-term security and family needs. Janet's executive-level business experience has given her an in-depth understanding of the unique financial planning requirements of time-challenged corporate executives and business owners.

Janet is co-owner of Dedicated Financial Solutions and is also a financial advisor with a Canadian investment dealer. She is a former director of the tax and accounting division of one of Canada's foremost publishers of taxation information for legal and accounting professionals. She serves on the board of the Etobicoke CA Association and is on the board of the Volunteers of Trillium Health Centre.

Janet and her husband, Zito, have made their home in Etobicoke for over 30 years, where they raised two children. Janet enjoys travel, golf, tennis, theatre, music and the company of her two granddaughters.

CPA = Chartered Professional Accountant
CPCA = Certified Professional Consultant on Aging
FCSI = Fellow of Canadian Securities Institute
FMA = Financial Management Advisor

For additional questions or to discuss your specific situation, contact us today to schedule your free 30-minute call.

Dedicated Financial Solutions
714 Burnhamthorpe Rd. E.,
Mississauga, ON Canada L4Y 2X3

Telephone: 905-896-8373
Toll free: 1-866-552-9333

info@dedicatedfinancialsolutions.ca

To book Janet and Jennifer for a speaking engagement, contact info@dedicatedfinancialsolutions.ca or go to www.createwealthnow.ca/speaking.

To order additional copies of this book go to
www.managingalone.ca or
use the order forms at the back of this book.

Introduction

Widowhood is not limited by age or gender. It can happen to both men and women, young and old, in a variety of circumstances. This book is meant for anyone who must now cope on their own, without their life partner's help and support. Widowhood is of course common for older people, but it is not unusual for people in the prime of life to find themselves, very possibly with young children, the lone survivor of what they had planned as a lifelong relationship. And it's not unusual for widows and widowers of any age to find themselves suddenly faced with a staggering number of questions and decisions to make about their financial situation, even if they had made some plans and financial arrangements in advance. For many people who have lost their spouse, the overwhelming sense of loss is compounded by a feeling of financial helplessness and uncertainty.

If it happened to you, would you be prepared? Would you know what to do?

Most of our clients are like the people in this book – intelligent, capable, competent people, but not always completely aware of their financial situation. Some of the widows and widowers featured in this book spent the better part of their adult lives with their financial affairs being managed by their spouse. It was a system that worked well until one partner was suddenly no longer there.

Our North American culture isn't comfortable with the subject of death, and few of us know how to cope with the pain of loss and grief. We're rarely encouraged to express our sorrow, so we've learned to control our feelings and to hide our pain. So it's natural that you may be reluctant to turn to friends, family and others for help – both with your emotional distress and your financial worries. This discomfort with and fear of death also makes it very difficult for people to discuss death and plan for it – avoiding those topics is extremely common. But addressing them can make the situation much easier for those who are left behind.

Each of us will handle the loss of a spouse differently, but we will grieve and we will need help. In the following chapters you will read about men and women who have lost a spouse. We hope you can relate to some of them and learn from their stories. As financial planners, we've worked with many widows and widowers and have grown to understand a number of issues they face.

Our website, Widowed.ca, came about after a friend's husband passed away. She first came to us for help getting life insurance on herself. During our meeting it became clear that the woman's young daughter was not receiving the Canada Pension Plan children's benefit – but she should have been. Over the next few days we tried to determine what had gone wrong.

It is very common for funeral homes to help with completing paperwork and forms at the time of the funeral. Although this can be a relief to a stressed, grieving spouse, it is not always the best solution and does not always cover the entire benefits process. And most people don't care to hear, right after their spouse has died, that they may be entitled to money as a result of that death. They'd rather have their partner back.

As well, immediately before and after the funeral, everything seems to be happening at once. The surviving spouse is overwhelmed and it's hard to take everything in. Even if they are told about it, often people don't truly "hear" or remember that they are entitled to financial benefits.

When we finally figured everything out for our friend, it turned out that, although the funeral home had completed and submitted the forms, the government had entered the information into its system incorrectly, and the payments to her daughter never began. Errors do happen, but if our friend had properly understood what her daughter was entitled to, she could have followed up and had the problem corrected much sooner.

Working with a professional who deals with these issues daily, whether it's an accountant or a financial planner, helps avoid such problems and makes it easier to correct them immediately if they do occur.

Once we cleared everything up, because it had been the government's error, the government provided the full amount of the benefits that should have been paid over those two years, with interest. The money was a big help – it enabled our friend to keep her daughter in her chosen school for another year.

We realized our friend couldn't be the only one who had had a problem with government survivors' benefits and Widowed.ca was born. When Widowed.ca began, it was purely a place where people could find out what government benefits they were entitled to. We wanted to make the information available so that people could get it whenever they were ready to hear the information, be it 10 days or 10 months after losing their spouse.

Since then we have grown Widowed.ca to include bloggers who share their own experiences of being widowed writing about different issues they have faced and also their triumphs in overcoming challenges. We have included links to trustworthy local resources for individuals to contact if they have a need – another problem our friend had mentioned was that she had had an accountant who made a mess of both her tax return and her husband's final return, leaving her in a very bad spot. She expressed that she had had difficulty finding someone she knew she could trust.

So visitors to Widowed.ca can now search for professionals such as lawyers, accountants, mortgage specialists and therapists from the resource pool we have built for our clients. The service providers listed there have been vetted through reference checks with their own clients. Once we had added these service providers to our website, we asked that they provide informative articles or blog posts that would benefit the widows, widowers and their loved ones who visit our site. The aim is to offer information provided by experts – they know their industry and services best and can educate our site visitors on how to deal with some of the issues faced by surviving spouses.

The most recent addition to Widowed.ca is a forum that allows widows and widowers to connect, to share and to support one another. Our focus is not on providing online grief support but rather on providing an open area for people who are looking to connect with others who are in the same situation. We have seen some very difficult stories on the forum and continue to provide as many resources as we can to help these people through their situations. Some of the most helpful information shared talks about things that work.

Our passion at Dedicated Financial Solutions is helping people. Widowed.ca allows us to help many people at once, many more than we possibly could in person. We hope to achieve that with this book as well.

About the Book

This book is an extension of our drive to help widowed people get on with their lives by offering resources, ideas, personal stories and financial advice. It's organized into chapters, each of which tells the story of someone who has lost their spouse. Each chapter focuses on two or three financial issues that are critical for that particular widow or widower, giving details on those topics. The book provides information on how to:

- Locate and access your deceased spouse's assets
- Learn what benefits the Canadian government provides to widows/widowers and their children
- Analyze your financial situation to help determine the best use of insurance proceeds
- Establish your own credit and financial identity, and why this is important
- Set up a trust to protect your estate
- Recognize unexpected costs of buying and selling a home
- Buy or lease a car with confidence
- Obtain insurance that provides the right coverage at the lowest possible cost
- Develop a financial plan that will protect your family if you die and allow them to live comfortably
- Plan for your retirement now that things have changed
- Deal with final expenses and your spouse's final tax return
- Go through the probate process and execute your spouse's will
- Manage if your spouse did not leave a will
- Update your will (and why this is important)
- Get your and your spouse's affairs in order when you know death is imminent

- Enter into business or loan arrangements with family members
- Choose advisors you can trust to help you accomplish these tasks

The topics of grief and emotional coping following the death of a loved one have been covered extensively elsewhere – and are not our areas of expertise – so we have not addressed those subjects here. We focus instead on financial matters following death. The More Resources section at the back of the book lists some books and websites that offer help with grief and the emotional side of widowhood.

10 Tips to Help You Cope

We talked to many widows and widowers before we launched Widowed.ca and before we began putting this book together. In addition to discussing their financial concerns, they told us about some of the things that helped them in the months and years after they lost their spouses. We would like to pass those suggestions on to you.

- If you don't already have one, get a companion animal and let your pet help you grieve.
- Touching helps. Take time for a massage.
- Talk to others who have experienced a similar loss – with them, you can express your sadness.
- Ask for help with tasks such as errands and repairs – people want to help.

- Let people know if and when you want to be alone. It's not personal, so assure them they are not being rejected.
- Find a place you can go for a good cry. Your feelings are normal.
- Use time when you are alone to remember, dream and think. Take time to process what happened.
- Identify your loneliest times and plan activities to keep you busy around those times.
- Realize that no one truly understands the relationship you had with your spouse.
- Let people know you want to remember – encourage others to talk and share stories about your spouse with you.

The 10 stories you are about to read are based on fact. The names have been changed, as have some of the details, to keep our promise of privacy to the people who have shared their experiences. We welcome your feedback or questions at Widowed.ca.

Jennifer Black
Janet Baccarani

Kayla

A New Start for a Young Widow

Kayla, age 25, and Jacob, 26, had been together from the time they were young teenagers. They met on the high school football field – he a football star and she a cheerleader. They lived for the fun of the moment but planned to go to college and then marry.

After the final game of the season in Jacob's last year of school, amid celebrations that included a few beers, Jacob and Kayla found themselves overwhelmed by the mood and by their love and things went farther than they intended. Weeks later, Kayla tearfully told Jacob the news: she was pregnant.

They married right away, college plans put on hold. No one but their immediate families knew their situation. Kayla was able to finish the school year hiding the truth, but as soon as school ended and Jacob graduated, they moved to another town. They didn't want anyone to know they "had to" get married. They even agreed to tell everyone their wedding date was actually a year before it really was.

They found a small apartment and Jacob got a job in an auto parts factory. Kayla enjoyed looking after him, packing his lunch and making dinner for them, and she busied herself preparing for the baby. But she had no experience with a household budget, banking or anything of the sort. Jacob took care of all that, and she had complete faith in him.

Jacob quickly got promoted, and they decided that he would forgo college. When the baby was born, Kayla delighted in caring for him; they knew they wanted more children. Two and a half years later, their daughter was born, and three years after that, another son. Jacob was promoted again – he was now lead hand for the auto parts shop he worked for – and was making a good living, with benefits, enabling the couple to purchase a house, albeit with a hefty mortgage and some help from their parents. Even so, Jacob was also able to put aside a little in a registered retirement savings plan with matching funds from his employer.

Kayla enjoyed her role as a stay-at-home wife and mother. She felt her role was to be there for Jacob and the kids and to look after their home. She still didn't know much about their finances – Jacob paid the bills, did the banking and handled everything financial. But Kayla now at least knew how to run the house on a budget. She was thrifty, sewing some of their clothes and doing all their home decorating herself.

Life for Kayla and her family was good. They had their own home, excellent health, good friends and family, and few money worries. Sure, they had to watch their spending, but as long as they lived within their means, life was good.

In the fall, Jacob enjoyed duck hunting with his friends. Early one Saturday, when their children were aged seven, four and the baby just six months, Jacob packed his gun, decoys, hip waders and a case of beer and kissed his wife and kids goodbye. He and the guys planned to spend the weekend in duck blinds and come home with the makings of some delicious duck dinners. Kayla was taking the kids to a local fun fair that afternoon to treat them to rides and cotton candy. It was going to be a great weekend for everyone.

On Sunday morning, there was a knock at the door. Kayla opened the door and was greeted by two grim-faced police officers. They asked Kayla to sit down and then explained that Jacob was gone. He had been wading out from the duck blind to pick up a duck he had shot. He had stepped into deep water and his hip waders had filled up, quickly pulling him under the water. His friends had not been able to get to him in time.

Just like that, at only 25, Kayla was a widow.

She collapsed when she heard the news. Her two older children came to her and tried to get her to stop crying, not understanding what had happened. Kayla had no idea what to do. She couldn't imagine her life without Jacob.

Her friends and family helped her through the days following Jacob's death and supported her through the funeral. But afterward she began to realize that she had no knowledge of her financial situation. The bank account was in Jacob's name and, when she went to the bank machine to get some cash, she discovered that it had been frozen because of his death. She didn't know about insurance, mortgages, bill paying or financial planning. She had no money – what was she going to do? The only work she had done since her children had been born was occasionally providing daycare and babysitting to other neighbourhood children, but this income was unpredictable and had never amounted to much. She and Jacob had never even reported these earnings for income tax purposes. Kayla had absolutely no idea how to run a household from a financial standpoint.

With a lot of help from a neighbour she began to sort things out, getting a better picture of her financial situation.

Financial Situation

Overall Financial Preparedness: ★☆☆☆☆

Jacob's Monthly Income: $4,500

Kayla's Monthly Income: Approx. $500/month from occasional daycare

---

Union Pension Plan: Jacob paid into it for 7 years; Kayla has no pension

Canada Pension Plan: Jacob paid into it from age 18; Kayla has not contributed (exempt before age 18)

RRSPs: In Jacob's name, approx. value $15,000; no beneficiary named

Other Investments: None

Bank Account: In Jacob's name, balance approx. $5,000

Life Insurance: $50,000 on Jacob from employer, naming Kayla as beneficiary; none on Kayla

House: Owned in Jacob's name; value $200,000; life-insured mortgage

Car: Late model; monthly payment $400, financed

Credit Cards: 2 in Jacob's name with life insurance on outstanding balances

Other Debts: None

Kayla's Credit History: No personal credit history, has never borrowed money, has not had her own bank account since marrying

Will: Jacob did not have a will

Main Issues for Kayla

After sorting through many papers with her, Kayla's neighbour urged her to see a financial planner who made her a list of the chief financial concerns she was facing.

Now that she was beginning to learn how personal and household finances worked, Kayla realized she was facing an even bigger problem: she didn't know if she had enough money to get by.

- Because Jacob had no will, it is more difficult to determine beneficiaries – the court must decide. Kayla will have to complete a number of forms and apply to the provincial court to receive a Certificate of Appointment of Estate Trustee without a Will naming her as administrator of the estate. She may have to pay an estate administration tax (probate fee). This process can take several months and can be expensive, because a notary/lawyer is required.

- Because the bank account was in Jacob's name only, at the time of his death it was frozen. Accounts in the deceased's name will remain frozen until the rightful beneficiaries are identified; then assets can be transferred to those beneficiaries. This process takes much longer if there is no will because of the court process of determining who the beneficiaries are.

- The frozen bank account, and Kayla's lack of income, meant she has no cash with which to pay bills and meet daily expenses.

- Jacob's RRSP was also frozen because no beneficiary was named, so Kayla could not cash it in to provide herself with some money for immediate expenses.

- Jacob's company life insurance did name Kayla as the beneficiary, and the insurance company paid it out within 10 days of Kayla notifying them of Jacob's passing. But Kayla didn't know the best use for the money – using it for funeral expenses, legal expenses and maybe paying off the car loan, or saving it to meet day-to-day expenses.

- Kayla needed to buy insurance to ensure that she and her children would be secure financially if she were unable to work, and that her children would be looked after if she were to die.

- Kayla needed ongoing financial planning assistance.

Kayla was greatly concerned that she would not be able to get by and look after her children. She didn't know whether she would be able to keep the house, but she didn't want to put the children through the stress of moving so soon after losing their father. She wondered if she would have to depend on her family for financial support. She did not want to be in that position.

Help for Kayla

Losing a spouse is enough of a burden without the additional stress of feeling helpless financially. Jacob's small life insurance policy was enough to cover funeral expenses and other estate costs but would not secure Kayla's future.

Kayla needed to see a lawyer right away to begin the process of applying for the Certificate of Appointment to allow her to administer Jacob's estate.

The financial planner urged Kayla to make an appointment with her bank. At that meeting she learned, to her shock, that the bank would not pay the mortgage life insurance. The bank said that the couple had not disclosed the fact that Jacob engaged in "dangerous activities." That, and the fact that he had traces of alcohol in his system at the time of his accident, voided the policy, they said. The bank reminded Kayla that if she were not able to meet the scheduled mortgage payments, they would foreclose on her house.

Kayla was in a panic. She had been counting on the mortgage insurance.

Accessing Frozen Accounts

To change ownership of Jacob's bank accounts and RRSP, Kayla needed to provide the bank with a letter of direction and Jacob's death certificate. A letter of direction is a letter from Kayla stating that she requires access to the accounts because they belonged to her spouse, who has just passed away. The letter had to clearly outline what she wanted done and must include the account numbers. The bank also asked her for a copy of her marriage certificate to prove that she was Jacob's legal spouse.

Kayla got the death certificate from the funeral home. They provided a dozen original copies of the certificate because many different institutions would require it. In addition to the bank, for example, the company financing the car would require one to transfer the loan to Kayla, and she would need to submit one with her application for the Certificate of Appointment.

Government Assistance for Widows and their Children

Kayla found the Service Canada website and worked her way through the paperwork to apply for the government funding for which widows and children are eligible: the Canada Pension Plan (CPP) provides a death benefit, survivor's benefit and children's benefits.

CPP Death Benefits

As Jacob's surviving spouse, Kayla can apply for the CPP death benefit. She should do so as soon as possible. She can get an application form at a Service Canada office (forms can also be found online at www.servicecanada.gc.ca and printed). Jacob's CPP death benefit was $2,050.

Many funeral homes will help with this process by completing the necessary forms and sending them off on behalf of the surviving spouse. However, if the widow or widower isn't aware that they are entitled to benefits, and if there is a problem or mistake with the application, causing no benefits to be paid, they may not realize they aren't receiving something they are entitled to. If the surviving spouse submits the application themself, they will know to follow up if the benefits are not correct or never arrive.

CPP Survivor's Benefits

CPP survivor's benefits are paid to the surviving spouse (including a common-law spouse), dependent children, or both, of someone who contributed to the Canada Pension Plan or who was receiving CPP retirement benefits. Children must be under 18, or under 25 if they are enrolled in school full time.

Eligibility for the benefit depends on how many years the deceased contributed to the CPP. Because Jacob had contributed continuously for nine years, Kayla was eligible for a small benefit. How much she would receive depended on Jacob's age and how much he had contributed to the plan over the years. The maximum amount a surviving spouse can receive changes each year; in 2013, the maximum spousal pension for those over 65 was $607 per month and for those under 65 it was $556.

Each of Jacob and Kayla's children can receive a benefit of $228 (in 2013) per month.

To apply for survivors' benefits, Kayla needed to get a Canada Pension Plan Death Benefit Application Kit from a Human Resources Canada Centre or from the funeral home. She could also get it by calling 1-800-277-9914 or online at www.servicecanada.gc.ca. She would also need the following:

- Jacob's death certificate
- Their marriage certificate (if they had not been married, she would need a statutory declaration of a common-law relationship)
- Jacob's social insurance number
- Social insurance numbers for her and the children (or their birth certificates, if they didn't have SINs)

Use of Insurance Proceeds

Kayla received Jacob's $50,000 company life insurance policy. Her first instinct was to put it toward the mortgage, after paying for the funeral, estate administration tax and lawyer's fees. The large mortgage balance frightened her and she wanted to improve her chances of keeping her house. But the financial planner advised her to first look at all her expenses to help her find the best use for the money. If she paid down the mortgage, she would tie up cash she could otherwise use to relieve immediate cash flow problems. The planner helped her calculate what the difference would be between putting the cash on the mortgage, and therefore having a lower monthly mortgage payment, and having a higher payment but also having cash on hand for day-to-day – and unexpected – expenses.

The planner talked with Kayla about her expenses and did a cash flow analysis. Her expenses included the mortgage payment and all the expenses of running the house: property taxes, maintenance, home insurance and utilities (water, gas and electricity). There were also cable television, telephone (land line and cell) and Internet bills and, of course, food. Kayla said they didn't need to budget anything for clothing for the first year because she could make do with what they had, making alterations as the kids grew and shopping at the thrift store when necessary.

Kayla said that the older children's activities – karate for her oldest, ballet for her daughter and swimming for both of them – were important and she wanted to keep them enrolled if at all possible. She didn't want them to have to give things up because of the situation. She wanted them to still be able to spend time with their friends and to participate in sports and dance. She believed sticking with their familiar routine would help them adjust.

Jacob and Kayla had had only one car, which she needed, but she agreed that she could find something more economical. Kayla said that she and Jacob had enjoyed going out and had quite often spent the evening at dinner or a movie. That money would now go toward the household budget.

Kayla and her advisor figured out that it made the most sense for her to keep what was left of the insurance payment on hand rather than put it toward the mortgage. She knew she would have to get a job as soon as she could, and therefore believed she would be able to carry the mortgage, but needed cash now, while Jacob's accounts were still frozen, government benefits hadn't begun and she wasn't working.

Conclusion

Fortunately, Kayla had friends and family to support her, to help her get back on her feet and to help her learn how to survive without her husband and partner. It was a long and difficult journey for her and her children.

Several years after Jacob's death, Kayla remarried. Her second husband adopted her children and they began a new life as a new family. Kayla's experiences following

Jacob's death made her determined to plan better for her new future, even though she and her new husband were young, healthy and financially comfortable. She knew she could no longer assume the worst would never happen. As soon as they were married, they met with a lawyer, a financial planner, an accountant and an insurance agent and made sure that if the unexpected happened again, they would at least be protected from financial hardship.

Planning for the Future

Kayla was determined, this time, to be more aware of and involved in their financial affairs. As part of their financial planning, Kayla and her new husband did the following:

- **Opened joint bank accounts.** Doing so ensures that the accounts won't be frozen, meaning the surviving spouse immediately has access to cash for daily expenses.
- **Switched the ownership of Kayla's house to joint ownership.** If assets are jointly owned with right of survivorship, they do not form part of the deceased's estate but instead pass automatically to the joint owner. This means probate fees will be reduced.
- **Made beneficiary designations on registered retirement accounts and pension plans.** Doing so speeds up payment of benefits and transfer of assets to the surviving spouse, without the asset being subject to probate fees as part of the estate. Talk to the financial institution that holds your RRSPs about naming a beneficiary

for your registered plans. If you are the beneficiary of your deceased spouse's RRSP, it can be rolled into your RRSP tax-free. Your employer's human resources office will be able to help you with naming a beneficiary for your company pension and life insurance.

- **Purchased life and disability insurance and named beneficiaries.** Naming beneficiaries speeds up payment of life insurance benefits and protects them from probate fees: when a beneficiary is named, the insurance proceeds pass directly to the beneficiary and do not form part of the estate. Life insurance enables your beneficiaries to pay your final taxes, probate fees, funeral costs, debts and mortgage, rather than using the rest of your estate for these expenses, and of course replaces your income to provide for your family. You need enough insurance to ensure that your family is financially secure without your income.

The financial advisor told Kayla and her new husband that having enough life insurance from a private insurance company to cover the mortgage was a better bet than getting mortgage insurance through the bank. As Kayla had experienced, with bank mortgage insurance, the surviving spouse does not know until after a death whether the bank would pay out the insurance or not. A private insurance company will make those underwriting decisions at the time you apply for the insurance. As well, private life insurance allows the beneficiary to decide what the proceeds will be used for, whereas bank mortgage insurance can be used only for the mortgage. Funds are needed almost immediately for funeral expenses, and private insurance can cover those.

- **Drafted wills and powers of attorney.** Having an up-to-date will makes things much easier for the survivors when someone dies, speeding up all claims for benefits, and of course ensures that the deceased's wishes are respected. Without a will, your assets are divided up according to the law. A power of attorney ensures that if you are unable to make financial or health decisions, someone you trust has the power to decide on your behalf and to carry out financial tasks for you.
- **Set up automatic bill payment from a joint bank account.** This way, they know the bills will be paid no matter what happens.

Points to think about that may apply to me:

_____

_____

_____

_____

_____

_____

_____

_____

Questions about my situation and whether something may apply to me:

_____

_____

_____

_____

Questions to ask my advisor:

_____

_____

_____

_____

Walter

Protecting a Legacy

Walter, age 62, and Anita, 60, had been very happily married for 35 years. Walter was a private pilot specializing in executive charters and therefore travelled extensively. Anita greatly enjoyed her part-time work as an event planner. They met when Anita was part of a group travelling overseas for a corporate event. Walter and Anita were very different but perhaps that was why they each truly felt that the other completed them.

They quickly settled into married life and had three children, proud that they could provide their children with so much. In fact, Walter felt they spoiled the children perhaps a little too much. As the children grew, their home became a focal point for their children and their children's friends – there was always a pool party, a barbecue or a sleepover happening.

Their children were now grown and were professionals whose careers were taking them to the executive level. Two of their children lived in distant cities, but family was important and they visited often. Walter and Anita had no grandchildren yet, but both hoped for the day when they would. Both enjoyed excellent health and took care of themselves to ensure that continued.

Because Walter was so frequently away, Anita took care of their well-appointed home and coordinated their active social life. The couple was highly visible in their community, both of them sitting on volunteer boards and participating in church and charity events. They had a large circle of friends and entertained frequently despite Walter's schedule. They enjoyed gourmet cooking – Walter was particularly accomplished. Walter and Anita also owned a large property on a lake where they had built a spectacular cottage and where they kept their boat, a motor yacht that could accommodate overnight guests. Family and friends gathered there frequently.

Walter and Anita were financially savvy. They worked regularly with a financial planner/investment advisor and with an accountant. The pair had built up a large investment portfolio and had ensured that they had made proper beneficiary designations. They had ample insurance and their wills were up to date. They felt they were prepared in the event of either of them being left alone, but couldn't imagine that coming to pass for many years.

One summer evening, Anita began to feel ill. She had a bad headache and a stiff neck, both very unusual for her. She took some pain relievers and headed to bed. Later that night, Walter awoke and could feel the heat of a fever radiating from Anita's body. He could barely rouse her, and when he did, she was disoriented. He called an ambulance. At the hospital, tests were done and IVs inserted while Walter stood by in confusion. He watched in horror as Anita experienced a seizure.

Hours later, the doctor told Walter that Anita had bacterial meningitis and that it was extremely serious. Her body was being flooded with antibiotics, but she was not improving.

Walter called their daughter, who lived close by, and sat with her by Anita's bed through the following hours, clutching Anita's hand. But, Anita did not survive. Walter was devastated. He could not bear to call his other two children, leaving the awful task to his daughter.

Walter was bereft. His family was there for him a great deal in the beginning, but they had to get back to their careers and, eventually, Walter was alone in his big house. He no longer enjoyed his beautiful home and gardens and didn't feel like going to his cottage anymore. It seemed pointless. Anita had always been there to share it all with him, and now she was gone.

Walter eventually returned to work, but he was dispirited and truly lonely. After 35 years in a joyful marriage, he couldn't bear to be on his own. With gentle pressure from his children, he rejoined a few community activities, just to get out, but returning to the empty house was heartbreaking every time. Sooner than he would have imagined possible, he found himself wanting to find a woman to share his life. Dating services weren't what he was looking for. He let people at his church and in the community know that he didn't want to be alone for the rest of his life. As a result, he found himself invited to events at which single ladies were also present.

Financial Situation

Overall Financial Preparedness: ★ ★ ★ ★ ★

Walter's Monthly Income: $12,500

Anita's Monthly Income: $6,700

Company Pension Plan: None

Canada Pension Plan: Walter has paid into it from age 18; Anita paid into it from age 20

RRSPs: Total valued at $650,000, each other designated as beneficiaries

Other Investments: Approx. value, $1.8 million, jointly held

Bank Accounts: Joint accounts; balance approx. $15,500

Life Insurance: $200,000 on Anita, with Walter named as beneficiary; $1,000,000 on Walter with Anita named as beneficiary

House: Joint ownership with right of survivorship; value $900,000; mortgage-free

Cottage: Joint ownership; value $600,000; mortgage-free

Vehicles: Motor yacht in Walter's name, approx. value $1.7 million, $50,000 mortgage, monthly payments $1,200; 2 late-model cars, monthly payments total $900

Credit Cards: Both had 2, plus 1 joint, balances paid off monthly

Other Debts: None

Walter's Credit History: Excellent

Will: Anita had a will naming Walter as executor and leaving all her assets to him

Main Issues for Walter

Walter's biggest challenge was not financial, it was emotional. A man's spouse is often his primary source of social support. Walter and Anita had been best friends and true partners as well as husband and wife – he had depended on her to keep the social side of their life in full swing. They had done everything together and he simply couldn't enjoy anything on his own. He was lonely and missed having a woman in his life. He also didn't want to lose his relationship with his social community now that Anita was gone. He began actively searching for a partner.

Walter's children became concerned. Because Walter's estate was quite large, they feared someone might try to take advantage of a grieving spouse. The family had always communicated well, so the children approached Walter to discuss their concerns. They wanted to put something in place that would protect the estate and their father from anyone unscrupulous. Walter agreed that this was wise: he did not want to lose all that he and Anita had built – and all that they had intended to pass on to their children, their future grandchildren and to charity. He sheepishly admitted that he had not even updated his will since Anita had passed away.

Walter wanted to make sure that any new woman in his life would not be expecting to share significantly in his estate – or worse, planning to divorce him for a large settlement or expecting to inherit it all when he died.

Help for Walter

Working with his accountant, lawyer and financial planner, and in consultation with his children, Walter decided to set up a trust to protect the estate. This was a good choice for Walter because his estate had considerable value – a large home, a valuable cottage property, an expensive boat and a significant investment portfolio. With a trust, Walter would have access to his wealth, but virtually everything he owned would be placed in the trust so that it would not be vulnerable to an avaricious new partner. He also needed to update his will and power of attorney, always essential after the death of a spouse.

Updating the Will and Power of Attorney

Whether Walter were to decide to marry again or not, it was critical that he update his will immediately to make his wishes for his assets very clear. If he were to remarry, he would have to revise his will again after the wedding to make his intentions clear because marriage automatically voids an existing will.

Inheritance rules, especially for common-law spouses, vary from province to province. In Ontario, for example, common-law spouses do not have the right to inherit and must sue the estate to receive anything. But in British Columbia, a common-law spouse has the same rights as a legally married spouse. If Walter were to remarry but did not update his will, it would become invalid and his new wife would automatically have a right to a significant portion of his estate, even though that's not what Walter wanted.

A clear, valid will was therefore the best way to ensure that the only people who would benefit from Walter's estate were those he intended to benefit – his children, future grandchildren and favourite charities. Having a carefully written and properly executed will would also reduce the chances that the will could be successfully contested by a new wife or partner who felt slighted.

In addition to revising beneficiaries to reflect the fact that Anita had passed away, he also needed to name a new executor. After speaking with his children, Walter chose his daughter because she lived nearby. It's important when choosing only one child of several to have an open discussion about it. Executors can be compensated for the considerable work they do, so when it comes time for the one child to be compensated it's important that the whole family feels comfortable with that. An open discussion will help.

Updating his will was simple: he talked with his children and his lawyer, the lawyer drafted the changes Walter needed to make, and the will was witnessed and signed. Walter left a copy with the lawyer, kept a copy at home and gave a copy to his daughter.

Walter's lawyer also took care of updating Walter's power of attorney for financial and health affairs because his current one gave Anita power to make those decisions if Walter were incapacitated. Walter appointed his daughter to this role as well – she was close by and could quickly get access to his documents, accounts or whatever was needed, and could be present at a hospital to make decisions, if necessary. He then created a living will, or personal care directive, outlining his preferences for care at the end of his life, again leaving a copy with his daughter. These steps would also help protect Walter if a future partner had designs on his estate.

Setting up a Trust

Walter's goal in setting up a trust was to transfer owner-ship of his assets to his children to protect the assets from being sought by Walter's potential new partner. Another benefit was that, with a trust in place, estate administration tax (probate fees) would be reduced on Walter's death – because the assets were no longer his, but rather were held by the trust, they would not form part of his estate and therefore probate fees, which are based on the value of the estate, would be lower.

There are two main types of trusts:

- A **living (inter vivos) trust**, which is created during your lifetime and begins operating as soon as you transfer your assets to it, allows you to maintain con-trol of your assets, but ownership of them is trans-ferred to your beneficiaries.
- A **testamentary trust**, which is created by your will, comes into effect when you die. The trustee looks after the assets and provides them to the beneficiaries ac-cording to what the trust documents say.

A trust is started by the creator placing a token piece of property in the trust. Your lawyer will draw up trust doc-uments that spell out who the beneficiaries are and when and how assets are to be distributed to them, exactly what assets are covered by the trust, who the trustee is (it can be a group of people) and what power the trustee has been given, among many other legalities.

Walter set up a discretionary living trust. His beneficiaries were his three children and future grandchildren. The assets to be included were his house and cottage; his cash accounts and investment portfolio; the proceeds of his life insurance policy; and his vehicles. The trust documents allowed for the sale of assets, such as vehicles, house or cottage, if none of the children wanted to keep them; for now, the family agreed to continue sharing the cottage and boat. Walter himself was to be the trustee during his lifetime. His children would take over as trustees once he passed away.

The trust protected his estate by transferring ownership of his assets to his children. Because he no longer owned the assets, a new wife or partner would have no inheritance claim on them when Walter died. The trust was discretionary, so Walter would have access to his property, assets and accounts when, and how much, he chose. This would allow him to give some of the money to one or more of the children at any time. And with the trust being fully discretionary (meaning none of the children has an absolute interest), if any of the children found themselves in financial difficulty, their creditors could not attack the trust assets.

Conclusion

Walter began to find that it was getting easier to interact with people while volunteering and at social events. He met some women who shared his interests in cooking and cottage life and whose company he enjoyed. Before a friendship progressed to dating, he always explained that the family had put a trust in place so that no part of his estate would pass to a new wife. She and Walter would live well together, but in the event of his death, the trust – and his assets – would be in the hands of his children.

Walter discovered, to his dismay, that one or two of his new friends lost interest when he explained the financial situation, but this served to confirm that he had been wise to put the trust in place. It was difficult to find someone, but through perseverance Walter did meet a woman – Caroline, a widow herself – who was happy to honour Walter's wishes for his estate. She wasn't interested in his assets.

Caroline also had grown children and wanted her assets to pass to them, rather than Walter or his family. She and Walter also talked about Walter's home. When Caroline had moved into Walter's house with him, she had sold her family home and put the proceeds in trust for her children. The new couple wanted to ensure that even though his house was destined for Walter's children, Caroline would not have to move if Walter died, unless she wanted to.

To accommodate his wishes with regard to the house, Walter and his children again met with their lawyer and amended the trust documents to create a separate trust for the house, granting Caroline a life interest in the home – she could remain there as long as she wanted without having to pay Walter's children. This gave Caroline flexibility and saved her from having to make a difficult decision during such a stressful time. When Caroline passed away or no longer wanted to stay in the house, Walter's children were free to do with it what they chose.

Walter and Caroline began to contemplate marriage while they enjoyed their remaining years together.

Points to think about that may apply to me:

_____

_____

_____

_____

_____

_____

_____

_____

_____

Questions about my situation and whether something may apply to me:

_____

_____

_____

_____

Questions to ask my advisor:

_____

_____

_____

_____

_____

Gabrielle

Establishing Your Financial Identity

Gabrielle and her husband, Bernard, both 52, were immigrants. They came from Europe with their young son, Marcus. When they arrived in Canada, they found a tiny apartment. Gabrielle worked in a hotel laundry and her husband worked in a factory. This was not the kind of work they loved, but they worked hard to establish themselves in Canada and to ensure they would have a home for their growing son. Gabrielle had a history of miscarriages, so Marcus was to be their only child.

Though she was highly intelligent, Gabrielle wasn't well educated and her ability to read English was not as strong as Bernard's, so her husband handled all the paperwork involved in running a household: insurance, banking, bills and so on. As time went by, they saved enough money to buy a house in the city. They rented out a couple of the rooms to help them manage the mortgage payments. They struggled, worked hard and eventually became financially secure. Bernard didn't know much about investing, so he bought some bonds and simply banked the rest of their money. Gabrielle was not very knowledgeable about their finances and didn't want to be; she always simply handed her paycheque to her husband. She knew he would look after her. Gabrielle knew how to run a house economically, and that helped them save money. They were young, healthy and moving ahead.

The couple didn't talk about money much and they had never met with an accountant or had advice from a financial planner. One of their neighbours worked for an insurance company, and after chatting with him, Bernard decided to buy some insurance for himself. Both Gabrielle and Bernard had company benefits as well; they felt they had nothing to worry about.

As Marcus grew, both Gabrielle and Bernard felt the pull of the land – both came from agricultural backgrounds and they longed to return to farming. They began to look for a piece of land and soon found one in the Niagara Peninsula – a fruit farm, where they could raise their own fruit and vegetables and even keep a few chickens. They sold their house in the city and bought the property. They had a small mortgage on the farm and believed that paying down that mortgage was their most important financial goal.

The family loved living and working on the farm, and did well, but they quickly discovered that they couldn't manage on the income the farm generated. Bernard had to find part-time work to supplement their income. Because he was a skilled machinist, it wasn't difficult for him to find employment.

Life on the farm was hard work but Gabrielle, Bernard and Marcus, now in his late teens, loved the outdoors and working the land. While they didn't have a great deal, they had each other and their good health – they lived a good life, didn't smoke or drink, and got plenty of exercise. Gabrielle managed the farm and greatly enjoyed dealing with buyers and suppliers, but she hadn't taken the time to improve her English reading over the years so Bernard still handled everything related to banking, finance and security. Bernard's employer provided health benefits, so they felt they were well looked after. They had never discussed wills and it had never crossed Gabrielle's mind that this might be something they should consider doing.

One February day, Gabrielle did the few chores required on the farm during winter, made a big pot of soup and waited for Bernard to come home from work. Their dog waited patiently in the driveway, knowing that when the car pulled in there would be treats for him from the leftovers of Bernard's lunch.

Long after dinnertime, Bernard had still not returned. Then, a phone call. It was Bernard's supervisor. Bernard had been involved in an industrial accident and Gabrielle needed to go to the hospital immediately. Gabrielle didn't drive, and her son was at his after-school job. But she called a neighbour and was soon on her way to the hospital.

Gabrielle arrived at the hospital, and the news was the worst. Bernard had not survived. A tow motor had over-turned right beside his workstation, dumping 1,200 pounds of cardboard directly on him. He had been crushed. Gabrielle was beyond distraught. She called Marcus but could barely explain what had happened.

The funeral had to be arranged and people had to be notified, but beyond that, Gabrielle had no idea what she needed to do. She knew that Bernard had been well orga-nized and kept all his important papers in a briefcase in their closet. Sorting through these papers after the funeral, Gabrielle and Marcus discovered that Bernard had life in-surance. They found half a dozen $1,000 Canada Savings Bonds and what appeared to be Bernard's will. But Marcus didn't know anything about his parents' financial situation either. Gabrielle didn't know the situation with the farm mortgage or what kind of benefits Bernard's employer might provide.

Gabrielle and Marcus needed help. Marcus thought the government had some sort of benefits for widows, but knew nothing else about it. Gabrielle was smart: she real-ized that unless she found expert help, they were in trouble.

She turned to her church and her neighbours and re-lied heavily on Marcus – everyone did their best to help her. But the more people she talked to, the more problems seemed to reveal themselves. For example, she didn't know if the will was valid, and the couple did not have a joint bank account. Because Gabrielle's English reading skills were very basic, she couldn't understand much of what came from the credit card company, the bank, the insurance company or Bernard's employer. She had to get Marcus to explain everything.

Finally, her priest recommended she see a financial planner and gave her an article about how to choose one.

Choosing Advisors

Gabrielle knew she needed help in many areas and was determined to gather a team of professionals to help her develop her financial independence. She would need an accountant, a lawyer, a financial planner and an insurance agent. She hoped to find an advisor who could combine at least two of those areas of service – financial planning and insurance, for example.

The right team of professionals can provide tremendous relief from the burden you will bear after the death of a spouse. You may simply inherit your spouse's advisors or ask for referrals from friends and relatives. These advisors may have been a good fit for your spouse or friend, but they may not necessarily be right for you. If you already have one or more advisors, think about what you know about them. Do they regularly contact you, or do you feel abandoned by them? If so, you may need to find new ones.

Questions for All Advisors

Whatever their specific role – lawyer, accountant, investment advisor or financial planner – all your advisors need to make you feel comfortable and let you know they are truly listening to your concerns and making your best interests a priority. Begin the selection process by asking friends, neighbours, relatives, colleagues, etc., for referrals. Interview several advisors for each role so you can compare them. You are essentially interviewing them for a job, and you are the one making the hiring decision. Ask all candidates the following questions:

- What experience do you have?
- What are your qualifications and designations? Have you taken additional courses? If so, why did you take those courses and how does this education help you serve your clients?
- What specific services do you offer? Can you give me what I need?
- Would I also need to work with someone else?
  - For example, if you are meeting with an investment advisor, you need to ask whether you would also need a financial planner and an accountant.
- Do you have a network of trustworthy professionals that you can refer me to for other advice?
  - For example, can a lawyer you are considering refer you to an accountant or financial planner?

- How will you keep me current and well informed? How promptly will you answer my questions? What procedures do you have in place to ensure timely updates and communication?
- How often will you meet with me to ensure that we are both up to date on my situation and to make any necessary changes?
- Who will I meet with in future – you, your assistant or any one of a group of people?
- How do you charge for your services (for example, hourly, by commission or per service), and what payment methods and schedule do you accept? What additional fees may there be, such as an account fee, customer fee or administration fee?
  - Ask for an estimate of average annual costs for someone like you.
- Are there any conflicts of interest I should be aware of?
  - For example, if the advisor is paid by commission, they may recommend products or services that pay higher commissions rather than those that are best for you.
- Have you ever been disciplined for unlawful or unethical conduct?
- Will you fully explain what you are doing and provide all information, plans and details in writing?
- Am I an ideal client for this advisor? Am I like many of your other clients? Do you specialize in helping people specifically like me? Do you understand my specific

situation? If I don't fit in with your practice, can you refer me to someone who is better suited to me?

- How many clients do you have? (You want to know if you are you one of 100 or one of 1,000.) Based on my assets, would I be one of your top clients or one of your bottom clients? (The answer will affect the amount of attention they give you.)

- Do you have any tools you've developed specifically to help your clients achieve their goals?
    - For example, they may have a website that includes resources specifically focused on helping particular types of clients – such as widows and widowers. Some advisors may have developed assessment tools to help you understand your own situation and needs.

- Do you prefer to meet at your office or will you come to my house?
    - Most financial planners and financial advisors will make house calls, but often accountants and lawyers do not.
    - If they have a preference, ensure you understand why.
    - You also need to know where you will be most comfortable. You may want to visit their office at least once to get an idea of how they operate and what kind of business they run.

You will also want to ask for current client references and follow up on them. Ask the references about the services the advisor provides. Ask the references some of the same questions about the advisor that you asked the advisor.

If it is important to you, you can also ask how the advisor contributes to the community.

Specific Questions for Financial Planners and Investment Advisors

- What are you licensed to sell – mutual funds, insurance, stocks, bonds? Do you offer true financial planning or are you simply an investment broker? Will you develop a comprehensive financial plan for me?
- Can you provide me with a sample financial plan that you have prepared for someone else?
  - The advisor will remove all the specifics, but the sample plan will tell you whether the type of plan the advisor prepares will help you.
- Do you look at the full financial picture – investments, tax, estate and retirement planning, insurance? Do you offer one-stop shopping for these services or will I have to see other advisors for other areas?
- How are you paid?
  - Some advisors are paid direct fees by clients, based on a percentage of the value of assets that are handled, and some are paid commissions for products they sell (such as insurance and investments). Some advisors are compensated with a combination of those methods.
  - You need to know how your advisor is paid so you can be aware of whether they may be making

recommendations that may benefit them more than they benefit you.

- What costs can I expect? How much are your fees and commissions? What other costs will there be – administration fees or fees to transfer assets from other institutions?
- Are you permitted to sell only one company's products or are you independent?
- Are you a Certified Financial Planner (CFP)?
  - This designation indicates that the advisor has passed a complex exam that deals with all aspects of financial planning: taxation, investments, insurance, and retirement and estate planning. You can also check whether an investment advisor is registered by visiting the Canadian Securities Administrators website and searching under Investor Tools.
- Are you an ELITE Advisor?
  - ELITE status is awarded by an independent third party, Accretive Advisor. Advisors can apply to go through the qualification process. As part of the process, Accretive Advisor surveys 100% of the advisor's clients. If the advisor's clients indicate they have a high degree of satisfaction with and trust in the advisor, the advisor will achieve ELITE status. To check whether an advisor has ELITE status, go to www.accretiveadvisor.com.

Specific Questions for Lawyers

- Are you interested in handling my concern or the task I need completed? Do you have the time to take it on?
- Do you have experience with the specific issue I need help with? What percentage of your cases are related to the issue I am facing?
  - If you need help with administering an intestate estate, you don't want a lawyer who specializes in criminal or real estate law.
- What size is your firm?
  - There are advantages and disadvantages to dealing with both large and small legal practices. In a smaller firm, you may receive more personal attention from your lawyer, rather than dealing with assistants or juniors. But a smaller firm may lack expertise in a specific issue you are facing.
- Will you outsource any aspects of the work I need done?
- Do you have malpractice insurance?

Specific Questions for Accountants

Chartered Accountants Canada provides a firm directory on its website (cica.ca) that allows you to search for accountancy firms by location, size, industry and services offered. If you don't have any referrals from people you know, you can generate a list of accountancy firms with the search tool.

- Are you a qualified chartered accountant as opposed to a tax preparer?
  - Tax preparers are not required to have accounting degrees or designations and may not be able to help you with a complex situation.
- Can you help me figure out what I need help with? Do you specialize in those specific issues?
- If you have a business: Can you serve my business accounting needs as well as my personal accounting requirements? Do you have experience in the type of business I have?
  - Not all accountants handle both business and personal taxes.
- Do you have liability insurance?
- As with lawyers, there are advantages and disadvantages to dealing with small and large accounting firms and with an individual. Think about whether you would rather deal with the same person each time, or whether it's more important to you to have someone available anytime.

How Do You Feel?

You also need to ask yourself some questions during the process of selecting advisors:

- Do you feel like the advisor is sensitive to your feelings?
- Do they listen to your concerns and answer your questions fully, in a way you can understand?

- Are you comfortable with the advisor and with their whole office team? Did you feel satisfied or frustrated after contact with the advisor or the office?
- Did the advisor encourage you to bring a trusted friend or family member to your interview?
- Did someone recommend this advisor to you? Would you have chosen this advisor otherwise?
- Do you trust the advisor? Are you confident their advice will be sound?
- Is this advisor appropriate for your specific needs, whether legal, accounting, financial or insurance?
- Do you feel like the advisor and the office staff understand your needs and genuinely see you as an individual?
  - Your impression can come from such things as the number of rings it takes them to answer your phone calls – and whether those calls are answered by a person or a machine – and whether people remember your name.
- Is it convenient to meet with them?

Gabrielle's experience dealing with suppliers for the farm helped her feel comfortable interviewing advisors. After getting some referrals and talking to some financial planners, Gabrielle selected one and made an appointment. Together they began to sort out the financial puzzle Gabrielle found herself in. She would then move on to finding a lawyer and an accountant.

Financial Situation

Overall Financial Preparedness: ★ ★ ☆ ☆ ☆

Bernard's Monthly Income: $3,000

Gabrielle's Monthly Income: $2,000 (farm income)

Company Pension Plans: Bernard paid into his for 20 years; Gabrielle paid into hers for 8 years

Canada Pension Plan: Both paid into it for 20 years

RRSPs: None

Other Investments: Canada Savings Bonds, value $6,000

Bank Account: In Bernard's name; balance approx. $3,000

Life Insurance: $50,000 on Bernard, with double indemnity for accidental death, but beneficiary is not named; none on Gabrielle

Farm: Joint ownership with right of survivorship, value $750,000; $80,000 mortgage

Car: Older model, fully paid for

Credit Cards: 2 in Bernard's name, outstanding balances approx. $3,800

Other Debts: None

Gabrielle's Credit History: Gabrielle has never borrowed money and has never had her own bank account or credit card

Will: Bernard had a will leaving all assets to Gabrielle, but an executor is not named

Main Issues for Gabrielle

In her meeting with the financial planner, Gabrielle said she knew she needed to learn more about financial management. She knew there was a lot to learn and that her reading skills were a problem, but she was determined and she was a quick study. She didn't want to become a widow dependent on her son, simply replacing Bernard with Marcus as her financial guardian. She didn't know whether she wanted to stay on the farm after Marcus reached adulthood and moved away, so for now she wanted to keep her options open. She wanted her son to build his own life and not have to be responsible for his widowed mother.

Gabrielle told the financial planner she felt stupid for being in the dark about her finances and apologized for the "mistakes" she had made. But the financial planner reassured her that her position was a common one and, although it wasn't ideal, it was perfectly normal for one spouse to be more responsible for, and knowledgeable about, the financial side of the marriage. However, it's a good idea to have periodic conversations so that both spouses know where they stand financially as a family.

Going through Gabrielle's papers, the planner discovered that the insurance policy Bernard had bought years ago would pay double indemnity (so $100,000) for death in an accident, but that Bernard had not named a beneficiary for the policy. That meant the proceeds would form part of Bernard's estate and would be subject to probate fees. So although she would receive the money fairly quickly because Bernard had a will, and she would be able to pay off the farm's mortgage with it, Gabrielle would have to set aside some funds for probate fees. Bernard's company pension survivor's benefit would also pay quickly.

Gabrielle and the financial planner identified these as Gabrielle's main concerns:

- The bank account was in Bernard's name, so it had been frozen until the death certificate was signed and the will was confirmed. Gabrielle had no cash in the meantime.
- She needed to apply for government benefits.
- The financial planner said the will appeared to be valid, but noted that it did not name an executor.
- Gabrielle didn't have a good command of written English or complex spoken English, so she needed someone to help her with these matters.
- Gabrielle had low financial literacy: she had never handled the finances and needed to learn how to complete day-to-day banking and financial management tasks, such as paying bills. Because of this, she needed to both improve her own skills and knowledge and select advisors who could help her.
- Gabrielle had never had her own bank account, credit card or loan, so she had a very limited credit history, based only on her joint ownership of the farm and the related mortgage payments. To be able to manage, she

would need to open her own accounts and apply for a credit card.

The planner believed establishing an independent financial identity and selecting the rest of her advisors were the most important tasks for Gabrielle's immediate financial health, and that a longer-term goal was improving financial literacy.

Help for Gabrielle

Establishing a Financial Identity

In addition to helping Gabrielle carry out the tasks below, her financial planner advised her on how to reduce taxes and recommended she see an accountant to complete her income tax return for her when the time came.

Opening a Bank Account and Line of Credit

The first step for Gabrielle was to set up a bank account and a line of credit and to apply for a credit card. Because of her limited English reading ability, Gabrielle preferred to visit the bank branch to open her accounts. Marcus accompanied her. She needed to take her social insurance card, another piece of identification proving her residency and proof of her income with her. She needed to list all her assets and liabilities.

At first, Gabrielle was overwhelmed by the many options for bank accounts, but she explained what she needed and the account manager recommended one for her. With

Marcus's help, she filled in the application form. She provided a small amount of cash, borrowed from Marcus, to open the account. When the funds from Bernard's account were released, they would be transferred to Gabrielle's new account.

The bank representative explained how the line of credit worked and how interest was calculated and told Gabrielle she could use funds from it immediately.

Marcus reminded her to ask about cheques. Though she was embarrassed, Gabrielle explained that her husband had taken care of everything financial and so she didn't know how to write a cheque. The bank representative again reassured her that she was not unique in this regard and showed her how to write cheques and to record them in her chequebook.

Applying for a Credit Card

Because Gabrielle and Bernard's house was jointly owned and the mortgage payments had always been up to date, Gabrielle had enough of a credit history to apply for a credit card with a small credit limit. Her financial planner explained that once she had the card, she should use it as often as possible for purchases she would be making anyway, and then to pay the full balance on time every month without fail. By doing this, Gabrielle would build up a good history of meeting financial obligations. A good credit history would allow her to increase her credit card limit, or to borrow money, if she ever needed to.

The bank provided Gabrielle with a credit card application, which she took home. She would need to provide information on her new bank account and to list her previous employment at the hotel laundry, plus her current work as a farmer. She would need to report her gross annual income. She would need her address history and to state that she owns the farm property mortgage-free (once the life insurance proceeds had arrived). The application asked about other debts, such as car payments or loans, which Gabrielle did not have.

Financial Education

As they left the bank, Marcus showed Gabrielle how to use the automated teller machine with her new bank card. She practised depositing a small amount of cash and then withdrawing it. Marcus wrote simple instructions for her for next time. At home, Marcus and Gabrielle figured out how to enroll in online billing for her utilities, and Marcus again wrote out instructions she could use to pay bills online. They then looked at a couple of utility bills and figured out how to pay them by cheque so she could choose the option that worked for her.

The account rep at the bank had told Gabrielle about a financial literacy course for adults that covered such topics as everyday banking, how to save and borrow money, and budgeting. Once they were home, Gabrielle and Marcus searched the Internet and discovered that the course was offered not too far from their home. Gabrielle called and enrolled for the next session.

Conclusion

As the months passed, Gabrielle began to feel ever more in control of her financial future. Her government benefits began flowing, allowing her to feel more secure, and she felt that every week she learned more about how to manage her finances. Marcus learned too, thus preparing himself for the day he would leave home and establish his own financial identity.

Gabrielle missed Bernard every day, but she was determined to be her own person, and being in control of her finances was a big step in that direction. She noted in her calendar when to schedule regular meetings with her advisors so that both she and they would always be up to date with her situation. For example, not long after Bernard died, she met with her financial planner to discuss life insurance, and she did so again when she was ready to begin saving for her retirement.

Points to think about that may apply to me:

_____

_____

_____

_____

_____

_____

_____

_____

Questions about my situation and whether something may apply to me:

_____

_____

_____

_____

Questions to ask my advisor:

_____

_____

_____

_____

_____

Sara

Final Expenses, Final Taxes

Sara, age 46; her husband, Mateo, 45; and their two children lived in a mid-sized city where employment was centred on the automotive industry. Sara worked in a bank, and Mateo worked for a major automaker, where he was a shop steward and active in the union. They owned a home, were active in their church and bowled in a league. The kids played hockey and piano and were involved in plenty of extra-curricular activities.

As a banker, Sara understood financial responsibilities and had seen cases where lack of planning had caused big problems. She knew how to manage household finances and understood the importance of insurance and saving for retirement. The couple had life insurance and had made wills. Sara took responsibility for most of the family's finances.

The family went on regular summer holidays, travelling throughout Canada and enjoying life to the fullest. Sara and Mateo felt they had everything going for them – a happy family, good jobs, secure finances and reasonable health. Mateo was a little overweight and he was sometimes short of breath, but he didn't think it was anything to worry about.

Life continued to be good for Sara and her family until one day Mateo collapsed at work. After Mateo was hospitalized, he and Sara met with their family doctor and a cardiologist. It turned out that his weight problem was something they needed to worry about – it was putting a strain on his heart. The doctors told them they needed to start looking after themselves better. If Mateo wasn't careful, and if he didn't make some improvements, he could have a big problem.

Sara put Mateo on a diet and encouraged him to exercise. She constantly worried about his health, but kept telling herself that he was still relatively young – too young for this to be a real problem. Mateo managed to lose some weight, and as time passed it seemed that everything would be fine. He went back to work – even putting in a few extra shifts to get a little ahead on the mortgage. Sara was working hard too and the kids were growing up.

One summer the family decided to take their holiday in the United States. They booked a cabin in the Adirondack Mountains and looked forward to a couple of weeks of exploring, fishing and relaxing. Four days after they arrived, Mateo collapsed on the porch of the cabin. He was gasping for breath. While Sara tended to him, their son called an ambulance. After a long wait for the ambulance to arrive at the out-of-the-way cabin, Mateo was rushed to the hospital.

The family sat in the waiting room, their hearts pounding, wondering if Mateo would be okay. Eventually a doctor came out to talk with them – Mateo would survive, but he had had a heart attack. He was going to have to stay in the hospital for a few days before they could move him. And he would need considerable time off work to recuperate.

Four days later, Sara arranged to transfer Mateo back to Canada by ambulance – at great expense. He remained in hospital for another two weeks and then continued his recuperation at home.

When Sara sorted through the mail that had gone unopened while she was at the hospital every day, she found the bills from the American hospital, cardiologist and ambulance service. The total took her breath away. Unfortunately, they hadn't taken out any out-of-country medical insurance for their trip to the US, and the medical fees amounted to more than $65,000. Their provincial health plan would cover only a small fraction of that. The bills depleted their savings but Sara was able to get a line of credit at the bank to cover the rest.

While Mateo was home on disability he got bored. Though he was supposed to be taking it easy, he decided to update their kitchen. He enjoyed the planning and he found a good kitchen company to do the work. He charged everything to the line of credit, knowing he would be able to pay it off quickly after he was back at work.

Eventually Mateo was well enough to go back to work. He was given lighter duties and fewer hours; life went back to normal. But then, just seven months later, Sara got a phone call from Mateo's supervisor. Mateo had been taken to the hospital. Sara raced to the hospital from the bank. Mateo was on life support and died shortly after she arrived. He had had a massive heart attack.

Sara was now a widow with two teenage children. Not having thought about a funeral, Sara didn't know what to do. She found herself wanting the best, the most she could do. She fell back on family traditions and arranged a big funeral similar to the one they had had for her father a few years ago. The funeral home personnel were very supportive and helpful with making the numerous decisions required.

Sara tapped into her network of family, friends and the union that had been a big part of her husband's life; everyone was very supportive. Mateo had had a will and insurance, and Sara had a handle on the family finances, but none of this helped her handle her grief or her children's anger that their father had left them – that was the hard part. And their planning didn't prepare her for the many decisions and arrangements she had to make following Mateo's death – or for the flurry of bills that began arriving soon after.

Financial Situation

Overall Financial Preparedness: ★ ★ ★ ★ ☆

Mateo's Monthly Income: $4,500

Sara's Monthly Income: $4,500

Company/Union Pension Plans: Sara had paid into hers for 23 years; Mateo paid into his for 25 years

Canada Pension Plan: Sara had paid into it for 25 years; Mateo paid into it for 27 years

RRSPs: Combined value approx. $45,000, each spouse named the other as beneficiary

Other Investments: Tax Free Savings Accounts, value approx. $50,000, each other named as beneficiaries

Bank Account: Joint, approx. balance $10,000

Life Insurance: $200,000 on each, with the other named as beneficiary, plus life insurance at work for 2× salary

House: Joint ownership with right of survivorship, value $350,000, with a life-insured mortgage

Car: 2 late-model cars, leased in Mateo's name

> **Credit Cards:** 1 in Mateo's name and 2 in Sara's name, paid off monthly
>
> **Other Debts:** Secured line of credit, balance approx. $110,000
>
> **Sara's Credit History:** She has a good personal credit history
>
> **Will:** Mateo had a will naming Sara as executor and leaving all assets to her

Main Issues for Sara

Sara and Mateo were intelligent people who understood the importance of financial planning. They had put into place everything they could to protect the family from financial strain if either of them died. Because everything was in order, the life insurance paid out quickly and everything – bank accounts, RRSPs, home ownership – transferred to Sara smoothly.

Despite this, and despite managing the household finances, Sara wasn't prepared for the aftermath of Mateo's death – the decisions, arrangements and extra bills. She even let some of them go overdue – she just wasn't mentally able to tend to them. She also became concerned about the line-of-credit debt. Another thing she wasn't prepared for was the increasingly frequent and angry phone calls from the finance company that held their car leases. Sara began to feel harassed.

A couple of months after Mateo's funeral, Sara sat down to take stock of the situation, to take care of the overdue bills, to get things in order and to begin to gather what she would need to prepare Mateo's final tax return when the time came. She needed to:

- Go over the final expenses to track them and make sure none were outstanding
- Deal with the car leasing company
- Prepare Mateo's terminal tax return

Help for Sara

Final Expenses

One of the items Sara had let slide was Mateo's credit card bill. When she found it, it was two months overdue. The balance – $6,750 – was higher than she expected as a result. They had always paid the credit card bills in full each month, so this lapse caused her to have feelings of failure. She paid if off and closed the account.

The next pile of bills related to funeral expenses. Sara had made many decisions about the funeral, with a number of service providers and suppliers, and she hadn't kept track of them all. When she gathered the bills and receipts, she was shocked at the total cost of the funeral.

The funeral home invoice listed the rosewood-and-brass casket Sara had chosen for Mateo, the undertaker's fee, the funeral home administration fees, and the reception room rental and staff for two visitations. She didn't even remember ordering the memorial cards the invoice showed, but she knew her mom had sent the cards out. She had receipts from their minister and the church organist for their fees for the funeral service. The church had also charged a rental fee for the reception hall for the wake, and there was the bill from the catering company for the food for the wake. Sara had ordered large flower arrangements for both the funeral home and the church. She had purchased a polished granite double memorial marker and had it engraved with both of their names, along with his union emblem. It was more expensive than she had remembered. The cemetery fee included the double burial plot, plus the fee for opening and closing the grave. Finally, she had written a long obituary for Mateo, but she hadn't even considered the cost of placing it in two editions of the newspaper. All told, the funeral expenses came to more than $18,500.

There was a bill from their lawyer for filing the application for a Certificate of Appointment with a Will – another $2,600. Probating the will hadn't been necessary because the assets were jointly owned or had beneficiaries named, so Sara at least didn't face any estate administration tax (probate fees).

Car Leasing and Purchase

Mateo and Sara had leased their cars because they liked to have new vehicles and so replaced them often. Both cars were in Mateo's name because it had been convenient to lease the two at the same time under one agreement. Sara had informed the leasing company of Mateo's death. She hadn't expected the leasing company to demand that she return their vehicles immediately, or the almost-daily phone calls from the company that followed, asking when the cars would be returned. Sara had told them that she wanted to simply transfer the lease to her name, but the company did not accept this and eventually told her they would tow the cars from her property if she did not return them within 24 hours.

Sara relented. Her children helped her clear their belongings out of the cars and she arranged for her brother to pick her up at the leasing company after she had delivered each car to them. She angrily paid the lease's early termination fee, yet another expense she hadn't counted on. Now she was without a vehicle, but she was so angry at the leasing company she didn't want to re-lease one of the vehicles she had just turned in.

Getting a new car was now another task she had to face. Mateo had been interested in cars and had always handled their vehicle purchases. There was a lot to consider:

- Should she lease or buy?
    - With leasing, you need to consider the monthly cost of the lease along with the buyout at the end of the lease. Purchasing reverses the cash flow situation: the down payment comes at the beginning, followed by monthly payments.

- Be sure to compare the cost of leasing with the cost of purchase financing to make sure you are doing the best thing for your situation.
- Compare interest rates. The leasing company (through the car dealership) can often offer a competitive rate, but if you have a good relationship with your bank you may be able to get a better rate through them for financing the purchase of a vehicle rather than leasing. It could cost you less in the long run and help you in the short term with your cash flow. Sara also had the option of using her existing line of credit to finance the purchase of a car.
- Lease agreements include a maximum allowable number of kilometres travelled during the lease period. If you exceed the limit, you will be charged a per kilometre fee. Make sure you know whether the number of kilometres allowed on your lease is enough for you. Think about the distances you normally drive every day, plus weekly trips and vacations, and multiply that by the number of years in the lease.

• Narrow your search to a few models, then read reviews of new and used cars in used car guide books, consumer magazines and online. Learn about problems that you may not have thought of and learn about reliability for each of the cars you are interested in.

- If you are buying a used vehicle, check car sales websites to get a sense of the value of the kind of car you are looking for so you are in a better position to negotiate.
- Take at least a couple of cars for long test drives – driving more than one will allow you to better compare and judge the ones you are considering. Can you see yourself driving that car every day? Will it work for long trips? Does everything you need to carry fit into it? If you have a garage or parking space, does it fit?
- Consider ongoing costs in addition to the monthly payments: insurance for that particular vehicle (ask your insurance company), fuel (does the car you're considering need premium fuel, for example?) and maintenance.

Terminal Tax Return

Five months following Mateo's death, Sara sat down to complete his final tax return. She had always prepared their tax returns because they were straightforward, so she didn't feel she needed to hire an accountant to do it for her, but she knew this one would be a bit different.

Sara had informed the Canada Revenue Agency (CRA) of Mateo's death at the time by calling 1-800-959-8281 and she had sent in a copy of Mateo's death certificate and will. She had ordered the booklet "Preparing Returns for Deceased Persons" (also available on the CRA's website at www.cra-arc.gc.ca/E/pub/tg/t4011/t4011-e.html). Because Sara is the executor of Mateo's estate, she is legally responsible for ensuring that his tax return is filed, whether she does it herself or has an accountant do it. If she wished to appoint someone else to be responsible for handling the taxes and dealing with the CRA, she could do so by completing Form T1013: "Authorizing or Cancelling a Representative."

If someone dies between January 1 and October 31, the final tax return is due by April 30 the following year, as it normally would be. If death occurs between November 1 and December 31, the final return is due six months after the date of death. Because Sara was Mateo's surviving spouse, the due date for her next tax return became the same as the due date for filing Mateo's final return. However, if she has a balance owing, she must still pay it by April 30 to avoid interest charges. (The due dates for final tax returns are different if the deceased or their spouse was running a business.) Sara had to report on her own tax return the CPP death benefit she received.

Sara gathered the T4 slips reporting Mateo's employment income and the pay for his unused vacation days for the year he died, plus his RRSP deduction receipts and income slips for his investments (T5 slips). Instead of filling in just his name on the tax return, she wrote "Estate of the Late" before his name and filled in his date of death in the appropriate box. Deceased people are not eligible to apply for the GST/HST credit, so she left that area blank. Otherwise, she completed the tax return as she usually did.

Sara signed the completed return as Mateo's executor and sent it to the tax centre. She had calculated that Mateo was to receive a small refund, which the CRA would make payable to Mateo's estate. Once she had received the refund and the Notice of Assessment, Sara applied for a Clearance Certificate by submitting Form TX19, "Asking for a Clearance Certificate," to the tax services office. This certifies that all debts of the deceased have been paid to the CRA.

Conclusion

After Mateo's death, Sara was more in need of emotional support than financial help. She was in reasonable shape financially and had no problem handling the family's finances, despite some concern about the line of credit. But she was grieving deeply, and her children were angry and hurt.

Sara arranged counselling for herself and for her children. They joined a group for families in the same situation and greatly benefited from talking with people who understood what they felt and who could help them get on with their lives.

Sara's experience arranging – and paying for – Mateo's funeral led her to talk with her siblings, her mother and even her teenage children about what she would like for her own funeral. She and Mateo had never discussed this; she had had no idea what he would have wanted. She felt she had gone overboard with Mateo's funeral, making needless arrangements under great pressure and emotional distress. She had purchased elements they could have done without. She realized now that she may have been subconsciously trying to show everyone how much she loved him. She had wanted the best for him, especially when it was the last thing she could ever do for him.

After her discussions with her family, she contacted the funeral home and, with a clear head, planned her own funeral, choosing the elements she wanted. She made arrangements to prepay with automated monthly payments on her credit card. For about $75 per month for 10 years, Sara would save her family from making decisions at the most stressful of times, as she had had to do, and from possibly overspending on the funeral.

She told her family about her plans and prepayment. She also added a page to her living will with information about what she had arranged and the contact information for the funeral provider.

Points to think about that may apply to me:

_____

_____

_____

_____

_____

_____

_____

_____

Questions about my situation and whether something may apply to me:

_____

_____

_____

_____

Questions to ask my advisor:

_____

_____

_____

_____

_____

Arthur

Taking Charge as Executor

Arthur, age 53, was a former member of the Canadian Armed Forces and a war veteran. He had married his high school sweetheart, Marjorie, now 52; they had a daughter two years later. But just after their daughter was born, the first Iraq war began, and Arthur's unit was deployed to the war zone. He was in the Middle East for two tours of duty, home briefly in between. When the war subsided, he was deployed to Africa on peace-keeping duty. He was later deployed to Afghanistan three times.

In his time away from home, Arthur formed a deep bond with his fellow soldiers. But when he returned home, he was greeted by a daughter he really didn't know who was growing up without him and a wife who increasingly seemed a stranger. They had to get to know each other all over again every time he came home. But he enjoyed being with his comrades. It sometimes seemed he spent more time with them than he did with his family when he was home.

Arthur and Marjorie had two more children – they felt their daughter would feel less alone with siblings. He and Marjorie quarrelled about the amount of time he spent with his friends and how she felt she was raising the children alone. They stuck together, but they both knew the spark was gone. Marjorie pursued her own interests too.

Partly in an attempt to save his marriage, Arthur retired from the military. He had a knack for numbers and understood personal and family finances, so he sought a career in the insurance business. He found a job that suited him and did extremely well. Insurance was something Arthur truly believed in. His military career had shown him that a family could be left without its income earner in the blink of an eye. He had also had a cousin, a man his own age, who had refused to see the value of insurance. His cousin had died suddenly, leaving his wife and four children financially devastated – no insurance, no company pension benefits, no savings.

Arthur made sure the same would not happen to his family. As a military spouse, Marjorie also understood the value of planning. Together, and in consultation with a financial advisor, they carried out proper financial planning and covered their bases by having ample insurance, naming beneficiaries and having clear, up-to-date wills. In their wills they named each other as executor and left all of their assets to one another. They named guardians for their children as well and, realizing that taking on the care of three children was a big financial commitment for their chosen guardians, they ensured they had enough life insurance to provide amply for their children's care. The insurance proceeds would go into a trust fund for the children, with the guardians as trustees.

The years passed, and Arthur and Marjorie's children grew up and left home. Arthur and Marjorie remained together. Their marriage was not the best, but they decided to carry on. Arthur continued to be busy with his work; Marjorie worked part time in a coffee shop. They had their own interests and friends and in many ways carried on separate lives. They shared a home and the occasional meal, travelled together sometimes and enjoyed hosting the children for the holidays. There was no animosity between them, just no all-encompassing love.

Marjorie gradually began to feel unwell sometime after her 51st birthday. She couldn't quite put her finger on what was wrong, so she put it down to age and ignored it. But when she began to experience a constant ache in her side and back, along with debilitating fatigue, she finally went to her doctor. The doctor sent Marjorie for blood work and abdominal scans. She was diagnosed with liver cancer. Her doctor referred her to an oncologist, who recommended diagnostic surgery. Marjorie was admitted to hospital within a few weeks for the surgery. But the oncologist did not have good news after the surgery: Marjorie's cancer was too far advanced to be successfully treated. The surgeon had reduced the size of the tumour to make her more comfortable, but the oncologist told Marjorie and Arthur that Marjorie likely had less than four months to live.

Financial Situation

Overall Financial Preparedness: ★ ★ ★ ★ ★

Arthur's Monthly Income: $5,000

Marjorie's Monthly Income: $1,000

Company Pension Plan: Arthur paid into his for 30 years; Marjorie had none

Canada Pension Plan: Arthur paid into it for 30 years; Marjorie paid into it for 14 years

RRSPs: $380,000

Other Investments: None

Bank Accounts: Joint, balance approx. $9,000

Life Insurance: $200,000 on Marjorie, $500,000 on Arthur, each naming the other as beneficiary

House: Joint ownership with right of survivorship, value $400,000; mortgage-free

Car: 2 late-model cars with monthly payments totalling $800

Credit Cards: 2 in Arthur's name, 2 in Marjorie's; paid in full monthly

Other Debts: None

Arthur's Credit History: Arthur had a solid credit history

Will: Each had wills naming the other and their children as beneficiaries and naming surviving spouse as executor

Although Arthur and his wife weren't as close as they once were, it was a shock to both of them. But they knew they had to prepare for Marjorie's death. Marjorie updated her will, power of attorney and living will one last time to reflect her situation. Hard as it was, together they planned and paid for her funeral. Marjorie's faith had played a big part in her life, and she was comforted knowing it would play an equally important role in her final service. Arthur was not a religious man, so with preplanning, Marjorie was assured the service would be as she wished. They both realized Arthur would have been uncomfortable, and out of his depth, planning a religious funeral. She took time to share her family memories with her children and her friends. The children came to stay with their parents in turns to help Arthur care for Marjorie as her health declined. In the brief time they had left, Arthur and Marjorie rediscovered a tenderness that helped them help each other through her final months.

Marjorie died at home and all of her wishes were honoured. The family held a thanksgiving for her life, not a marking of her death, as she had requested. The children received their legacies according to their mother's wishes. The bank accounts, will and insurance were all in order – the accounts were jointly held and so passed automatically to Arthur, the will was clear and valid and with Arthur named as beneficiary of the insurance, the policy paid to him quickly. A difficult time had been made a little easier with planning.

Main Issues for Arthur

Arthur and Marjorie had, to a great extent, led separate lives, but they had been united in their belief in financial planning and preparing for an inevitable death. They had enough care and respect for each other that they didn't want to leave the surviving spouse and the children in a financial mess. All that was left to do after Marjorie passed was execute her will.

As well, with the children grown and leading their own lives, and Marjorie now gone, Arthur began to wonder whether he needed to keep the family home they had had for many years. He certainly didn't need that much space and wasn't particularly interested in maintaining a big home and yard.

Help for Arthur

Executor's Role

An executor is someone you will never need in your lifetime, but who will be extremely important to your family after you die. As Marjorie's executor, Arthur was responsible for carrying out her wishes and distributing her assets as described in her will and for completing administrative, legal and financial requirements, such as filing her final tax return.

The selection of an executor is one of the first and most important considerations in writing a will. People often choose a family member, a trusted friend or relative, or a business associate to act as executor. An institution, such as a law firm, can also act as executor. You should also name an alternate executor in case the primary executor cannot take on the responsibility or decides not to. It is crucial to ask potential executors, both the primary and the secondary, whether they are willing to serve in that role and get their agreement before you name them to reduce the likelihood of a problem after you die.

At the simplest level, the executor's duties are the same for all estates, but depending on the complexity of a particular estate, the amount of work and the number of tasks will vary. Execution of very complicated or large estates can sometimes take years to complete. Regardless of the size of the estate, the executor takes on great responsibility.

Some of the executor's responsibilities are listed below.

Organize a Meeting

The executor should organize a meeting of the deceased's family to review funeral arrangements and confirm the whereabouts of insurance policies, investment statements, safe deposit boxes, share certificates, the will, and so on. Ensure that everyone who should be informed about the death has been told. If the deceased had pets that now require someone else's care, you must arrange for this immediately.

Locate and Review the Will

The first priority of an executor is to obtain the most recent original copy of the deceased's will – and determine which will is the latest one if there is more than one. Ideally, the executor will have been informed where the will is, or may even already have a copy.

If the will cannot be located among the deceased's papers at home, check for a safe deposit box. You will need to call the bank and make an appointment to open the box. The executor should take the key, a copy of the death certificate (a burial certificate issued by the funeral home may suffice) and identification. If the will is in the safe deposit box, the executor can confirm that he or she is indeed named as executor. The bank should allow the executor to take the will away with them. A bank employee will make a list of the contents of the box and give the executor a copy of the list. Ironically, a safe deposit box is a poor place to keep a will because of the potential difficulty in getting to it.

If the will is not in the safe deposit box or at the deceased's home, the deceased's lawyer should have a copy. You may have to look through the personal papers again to find the lawyer's name if you do not know it.

Once you have the will, determine with a lawyer whether it is valid and whether there may be any problems with it. Determine the complexity of the estate.

Arrange the Funeral

Assuming the funeral has not already been planned, one of your first major duties as executor is to assist with funeral arrangements. The executor will, no doubt, want to consider the wishes of the deceased, as well as those of the immediate family, as expressed in the will or elsewhere. Because Marjorie had planned and paid for her funeral, Arthur had few decisions and plans to make or bills to pay. He simply had to choose a date, inform the various service providers and suppliers, and book what was needed.

After the funeral, obtain several original copies of a funeral director's statement of death or provincial death certificate from the funeral home. If the funeral has not been prepaid, the funeral bills can be presented to the deceased's bank. The bank will give the executor an official cheque drawn on the deceased's account to pay the funeral home. Financial institutions will generally permit cheques to be drawn on the deceased's account, with minimal documentation, as long as these payments are for the funeral or for medical bills incurred immediately before the death. Beyond these strictly limited expenses, the financial institution will demand that all their documentary requirements be met before releasing any funds. Because Arthur and Marjorie had joint bank accounts, Arthur had no problems accessing funds – the bank accounts were still available to him.

Tend to Routine Financial and Administrative Matters

The executor must ensure the immediate cash needs of dependents are met. He or she must cancel all the deceased's credit cards (and destroy the actual cards), subscriptions, memberships, etc. Utility services may need to be terminated or account information changed. If Marjorie had been receiving Canada Pension Plan benefits or Old Age Security payments, Arthur would have had to terminate Marjorie's payments. An executor must also communicate with the deceased's employer, if applicable, regarding any back pay, vacation pay or pension benefits that may be available.

The executor is also responsible for submitting claims on any private life insurance policies that the deceased held. Arthur contacted their insurance company and provided Marjorie's policy number, her social insurance number, birth certificate, death certificate and his own personal information as the beneficiary.

Manage the Estate

Discuss with a lawyer whether probate is necessary. The lawyer will also help you apply for any needed certificates. The executor must first determine who the beneficiaries are, as indicated in the will, and inform them that they are beneficiaries. He or she must also prepare an inventory of all the deceased's assets. Assets that were owned jointly with another person, such as Marjorie and Arthur's home and bank accounts, or where a beneficiary designation had been made, such as with their life insurance policies and RRSPs, do not form part of the estate. In some cases it may be appropriate to open a bank account for the estate.

The executor must ensure that tangible assets, such as houses and vehicles, are secure and that proper insurance is in force. In particular, ensure that homeowners' insurance does not become void if the home is vacant. The executor also needs to compile a complete list of the deceased's debts (loans, credit card bills, utilities, property taxes, etc.) and arrange for these to be paid. If necessary or appropriate, executors should place an advertisement in a local newspaper asking creditors to come forward so that all of the deceased's debts can be paid. Do not make any disbursements to beneficiaries until all debts are paid.

After Arthur had gathered all the paperwork, he paid off Marjorie's credit cards and an outstanding vet bill for her dog, but everything else was up to date.

The executor needs to arrange for the sale of any property that the will indicates should be sold – Arthur sold Marjorie's car because none of the children needed it, and arranged to donate many of her personal belongings to charity.

The executor is responsible for ensuring that the deceased's final income tax return is filed, whether the executor completes it or hires someone to do so. After you have received the Notice of Assessment for the final return, you must request a Clearance Certificate (Form TX19, "Asking for a Clearance Certificate") and ensure that you receive it

– follow up if you don't. This certificate from the Canada Revenue Agency states that everything is settled regarding the deceased's estate and that there are no further taxes or other debts owed to the CRA by the deceased.

Make Distributions from the Estate

Payments for necessary expenses of the deceased's dependants may be permitted, but the executor should not make any distributions from the estate to beneficiaries during the first six months without the surviving spouse's written consent or an authorization from the court. In fact, the executor should wait six months before distributing any assets to the beneficiaries, even if there is no surviving spouse, because the deceased's dependents have six months during which they may contest the will. The executor may not make the final distribution of estate assets until the CRA has issued the Clearance Certificate.

A Certificate of Appointment of Estate Trustee with a Will (or without a Will), formerly called letters probate or letters of administration, is almost always necessary to transfer title of assets such as marketable securities and real estate. Financial institutions generally require notarized copies of the Certificate of Appointment before they will change the ownership of a financial asset or disburse funds to the executor. This protects the financial institution from liability arising from claims by other parties.

Keep Detailed Records

As executor you need to keep full and accurate records of all transactions into, or out of, the estate account. Keeping track of all personal disbursements you make in the course of your duties as executor is also important so that you may be reimbursed. As executor, you are allowed to be paid for the work you do for the estate. Make sure you keep track of compensation the estate provides to you for your time and effort. When the final distribution of the estate is complete, the executor should get signed releases from the beneficiaries absolving the executor from any further claims.

The executor can delegate any of these tasks to others, but the executor remains responsible for ensuring that everything is done properly, completely and as directed by the will.

Considerations in Selling and Buying a House

It had been many years since Arthur and Marjorie had bought their home. Arthur assumed things had changed since then and felt he didn't have a good understanding of the home buying and selling process. He got his financial planner to recommend a real estate agent, who went over the process with him.

They began by discussing where he wanted to live – in the same neighbourhood as he did now, elsewhere in the same town or in another town. He needed to consider proximity to his work and to his children. Next he needed to think about what sort of home he wanted – a smaller detached house with a yard, a freehold townhouse or a condominium townhouse or suite? How much space would he need?

The agent went over some of the costs that might arise.

The Cost of Selling

When selling, he would need to consider the following expenses:

- **Escrow, title insurance, mortgage redemption and other fees.** These vary considerably according to your individual circumstances, so do your research before putting the house on the market.
- **Legal fees.** At a minimum, you will need a final legal opinion on the purchase agreement. If you want legal advice throughout the process, legal fees could be substantial.
- **Real estate agents' fees.** The seller usually pays the agents' commissions.
- **Renovations.** Strategic renovations can increase the value of your property and perhaps more importantly improve the "showability" of your home. Experts suggest you pay the most attention to de-cluttering, painting (in neutrals), improving bathrooms and kitchens, and enhancing curb appeal. Hiring a stager may be a good decision as stagers can improve your home's look without making major (expensive) changes.

- **Repairs.** These may be repairs that are needed before you can list your home for sale. Or, once you receive an offer, there may be items noted in a prospective buyer's home inspection that must be completed before the buyer finalizes the agreement. Arthur's agent recommended that he have a home inspection done himself prior to listing the house for sale. It had been a long time since he had bought the house, and he and Marjorie had not devoted a great deal of their time or money to maintaining or improving the house.
- **Rent and storage.** If you sell your house before purchasing a new property, you may have to rent temporary accommodations for both yourself and some of your belongings.

The Cost of Buying

Some of the expenses associated with buying a house are as follows:

- **Home appraisal.** If you are applying for a mortgage, the lender may want to establish an independent fair market value for the home you are considering.
- **Home inspection.** This analysis will identify mechanical or structural problems and provide you with a list of recommended repairs and sometimes the estimated cost.
- **Moving expenses.**
- **Upgrading, decorating and renovating your new home.** You may have to make repairs recommended in the

home inspection if you have not required the seller to do them.

- **HST or GST.** Federal tax is payable on many of the services associated with buying a house, such as commissions, lawyer's fees and appraisals. It is also payable on new homes, but not on the purchase of resale homes.
- **Land transfer tax.** This varies provincially and is a percentage of the price of the property.
- **Lawyers' fees.** Mortgage lenders may require a lawyer to write and register the mortgage contract and you should have a lawyer review the purchase agreement.
- **Property taxes.** These are based on the assessed value of your property and the mill rate set by the municipality. In the purchase agreement there will be an adjustment date that establishes when the property taxes become your responsibility. You may have to reimburse the seller if they have prepaid taxes, or the seller may owe you.
- **Utilities.** Hooking up telephone, cable, Internet, electricity, gas, etc. may cost more than you anticipate.

Conclusion

Even though Arthur and Marjorie had not had the closest married relationship, they had been companionable. Arthur was used to being married, and he wanted to try again. He was still relatively young and in good shape financially. After he moved to a smaller townhouse, he began to look for someone to share the latter part of his life with. It took time, but eventually Arthur fell in love and remarried, five years after losing his first wife.

Points to think about that may apply to me:

_____

_____

_____

_____

_____

_____

_____

_____

_____

Questions about my situation and whether something may apply to me:

_____

_____

_____

_____

_____

Questions to ask my advisor:

_____

_____

_____

_____

_____

Aisha

Coping When There's No Will

Aisha, 43, and her husband, Ismail, 50, immigrated to Canada from Pakistan 10 years ago. They had six children. The two youngest girls, aged 11 and 14, were still in school. The next-oldest, a 17-year-old son, had just finished high school and was working part time, still living at home. The two older daughters and elder son were married, but one of the daughters, 19, was living with the family because her husband was back in Pakistan and she had four-month-old twins to look after. So it was a full and busy household.

At home in Pakistan, Ismail had been a senior factory manager. The family had been comfortable and owned a large home as well as another parcel of land. They had been able to save funds for a down payment on their home in Canada, so they had kept their properties in Pakistan, renting out the house. They came to Canada in the hopes of providing a prosperous future for all of their children.

Ismail had been working in assembly at an appliance plant for nine years. Aisha had taken a part-time job in the same factory after their youngest child started school six years ago, but had just been laid off temporarily. Their employer offered only a modest benefits plan. As part of the plan, Ismail had a small amount of life insurance. But because he had type 2 diabetes and was significantly overweight, additional coverage would have been quite expensive for him, so he stuck with the basic coverage. As a part-time employee, Aisha had not been entitled to any benefits. On their current income, and because of their large family and their mortgage, the couple had not been able to build up any savings, other than a small RRSP contributed to in part by Ismail's employer. Financial planning was not something they thought about at all – family life seemed to use up all of their energy as well as all of their income.

One Sunday, Aisha and Ismail were visiting their married daughter, Sonja, and son-in-law, Jared, at their new apartment. Ismail and Jared were out on the balcony, trying to remove some old pigeon nests along the outer edge of the railing. As Ismail stretched and leaned over the edge, he gasped sharply, cried out, and fell. Jared lunged toward him, but could not grab him in time. Ismail fell to the ground from the third-floor balcony. The family was screaming in the apartment. Some rushed down the stairs, and onlookers gathered below. An ambulance was called and Ismail was whisked to the hospital. Aisha and her family followed. But nothing could be done. Ismail was pronounced dead at the hospital.

The autopsy revealed that Ismail's death had been caused by a massive heart attack – he had died before he even fell.

Aisha's first and most sustained feeling in reaction to this turn of events was panic. She didn't know how she would manage – how the whole family would manage – without Ismail. The more she thought about it, the more afraid she was. She was sure they would lose the house, she didn't think they would be able to pay their bills and she worried that ultimately they would have to return to Pakistan, their children's future lost. Her children tried to reassure her that this would not happen, but she could not be convinced.

Sonja and Jared quickly gave up their new apartment and moved back into the family home to both help with the family expenses and to help Aisha manage. Sonja gently tried to help Aisha get some understanding of her financial position so she could begin to take control and reduce her worries about money.

One of the first things Aisha did was go to the benefits office at Ismail's employer to claim his life insurance. She ran into difficulties immediately: the representative told her that no beneficiary had been named so they would need to see the will, the death certificate and the Certificate of Appointment. Aisha's English was not as strong as she would have liked, and she wasn't able to understand everything that was said to her. She believed the representative was telling her she would not get the insurance and became quite upset. The representative was not helpful and simply repeated that he couldn't help Aisha until she produced the appropriate documentation.

At home, Aisha told her family what she had been told, and they gathered what they could of the documentation. Even this added to Aisha's sense of panic. Looking at Ismail's death certificate, she saw the cause of death listed as "myocardial infarction" and was sure it was a mistake, because the doctor had told her Ismail had died of a heart attack. Aisha was sure the mistake would cause more problems. It was only after one of the children did an Internet search for the term that they understood it was simply the medical name for a heart attack. It was a minor thing, and quickly resolved, but had added to Aisha's stress and worry.

Sonja asked Aisha about Ismail's will, since the benefits administrator at the factory had said they would need it, but Aisha said she didn't think Ismail had one. They were certainly not able to find one. This was another problem that increased Aisha's sense of panic.

Sonja was trying to help her mother sort everything out, but she was not experienced in financial matters either and finally recommended that they find a financial advisor who could help them sort through everything. Sonja accompanied Aisha to the meeting. The advisor began by taking stock of the situation.

Financial Situation

Overall Financial Preparedness: ★ ☆ ☆ ☆ ☆

Ismail's Monthly Income: $4,000

Aisha's Monthly Income: None at time of Ismail's death because of layoff

Other Income: Aisha's adult son, one daughter and son-in-law living at home now contributed a total of $1,800/month toward household expenses; $400/month rental income from house in Pakistan

Company Pension Plan: Ismail paid into his for 9 years but did not name a beneficiary; Aisha paid into to hers for 5 years

Canada Pension Plan: Ismail had paid into it for 9 years; Aisha for 5

RRSPs: $6,000 in Ismail's name, Aisha named as beneficiary

Other Investments: Rental property in Pakistan in Ismail's name

Bank Account: 1 in Ismail's name, approx. balance $2,500

Life Insurance: $100,000 on Ismail, no beneficiary named; none on Aisha

House: Joint ownership with right of survivorship, value $350,000 with a mortgage of approx. $200,000

Car: Late model car in Ismail's name, with monthly payment of $450

Credit Cards: 1 joint card, balance approx. $5,200, not paid in full each month

Other Debts: None

Aisha's Credit History: She has a history through joint credit card account and joint ownership of the mortgaged house

Will: Ismail did not have a will

Main Issues for Aisha

Aisha and the financial advisor agreed that she had many financial issues to sort out – Aisha called it a real mess. But the advisor assured her that in many couples the husband takes care of the financial side of things, with the wife managing all aspects of looking after the home and the children, so her lack of knowledge, though not ideal, was far from unusual. The advisor also told her that many people die without wills, so again, although it was a problem, it wasn't an unusual one. The advisor reassured her that they would get it all sorted out in time. The concerns Aisha was facing included the following:

- The most significant, and most urgent, problem was that Ismail had not left a will. Because there was no will, neither Ismail nor his surviving family had any say in what happened to his assets and personal possessions. The estate would have to go through the probate process.

- Beneficiaries had not been named on Ismail's company survivor pension or life insurance. Combined with the lack of a will, this made it very difficult for Aisha to access the insurance and pension.

- The bank account was in Ismail's name only and therefore was frozen when he died, until beneficiaries were identified. But with the bank account frozen, Aisha couldn't access the funds and was relying on her children's help for daily expenses. The invoice from the funeral home had not been paid.

- Ismail's life insurance policy was not sufficient to provide for his large family, especially as Aisha was temporarily out of work.

- Aisha had not been aware of the government assistance programs for surviving spouses and children.

- Aisha did not have any life insurance, but with dependent children and grandchildren, she knew she needed some.

- Aisha was not sure of her position and rights regarding the properties in Pakistan. She was concerned that the laws in Pakistan might make it possible for Ismail's relatives there to lay claim to the properties because they had been owned by Ismail, not Ismail and Aisha jointly. She was afraid she would lose them outright.

Help for Aisha

Aisha's case was complex and involved many issues that would take time – and money – to work through. Her financial advisor strongly recommended that Aisha meet with a lawyer as soon as possible to help her through the intestacy (lack of a will) situation and to clarify her rights regarding her properties in Pakistan. She would probably need to make contact with a lawyer in that country as well. This was not something a financial planner could help with, and it was not something Aisha and her family should try to handle on their own.

Her advisor recommended that Aisha get more copies of Ismail's death certificate from the funeral home – she would need them for the many applications and other paperwork she would need to complete.

The advisor made a list for Aisha of all the government benefits that she and her three youngest children (those under 18) were eligible for: the death benefit, CPP survivor's benefits and orphans' benefits. Together Sonja and the advisor helped Aisha fill in the application forms and then she mailed them off.

Dealing with the Bank

The advisor told Aisha that if she had the death certificate, Ismail's bank account information and their marriage certificate, she could go to the bank and ask it to pay the bill from the funeral home directly from Ismail's frozen account. Funeral bills are considered legitimate estate expenses, and most banks will pay them directly from the deceased's account to the funeral home if provided with documents proving the relationship of the deceased to the person providing the funeral bill. Getting this bill out of the way was a relief for Aisha.

Because Ismail's RRSP was relatively small (less than $10,000) and it named Aisha, his spouse, as the beneficiary, the advisor believed that the bank might be willing to transfer the RRSP to Aisha right away, even without a will or a Certificate of Appointment naming Aisha as administrator of the estate. The risk for the bank in making the transfer was low because the bank knew that when the estate went through probate and was divided according to inheritance laws, a significant portion would go to the spouse anyway. So, with the documentation she had, Aisha was able to have the bank do this. She felt a bit more secure knowing that there was a little money there as she needed it.

Aisha also needed to get access to Ismail's bank account. In addition to the documents she had already presented to the bank, she needed to give them a letter of direction indicating exactly what she wanted done. The bank would possibly require the Certificate of Appointment before giving her access as the executor. The bank would open an account in Aisha's name, and she would then have to direct all income to that new bank account and start paying bills from that account.

Aisha's financial advisor recommended the following for life insurance. Because cash flow was a concern and Aisha was not in perfect health herself, the advisor and Aisha agreed that just getting the minimum coverage was best for her situation. It was very important that she have some coverage because she still had two children who relied entirely on her financial support and a home that was not fully paid off. She needed enough insurance to provide the family with the financial resources to pay off the mortgage, giving them a home to live in, and enough money to raise the two youngest until they were 18. At that point they would be able to start working and contribute to the family financially if needed.

What to Do When There Is No Will

Because there was no will, Aisha had to go through a long process to settle Ismail's estate. This process can take many months and can be expensive because a lawyer is required.

When there is no will, there is no executor. That means the court has to appoint an executor. The surviving spouse is usually the first choice. If that's not possible or appropriate in a particular case, an adult child or grandchild may be appointed. A parent or sibling can also be appointed.

Wills are provincial matters. Because she lived in Ontario, Aisha completed, with her lawyer, an Application for a Certificate of Appointment of Estate Trustee without a Will, along with several other forms, and submitted them to the provincial courts. Once her application was approved, she would receive a Certificate of Appointment (formerly called letters of administration). This certificate would make her the executor/administrator of the estate. The application requires the following information:

- Information on the deceased: name, address, date and place of death, marital status and last occupation
- Names, addresses and relationship (and age if younger than 18) of everyone entitled to a portion of the estate according to the province's inheritance laws
- Net value of the estate's assets, including personal property worldwide and real property in Ontario.
  - Ismail's estate included the contents of his bank account, his life insurance policy (because no beneficiary was named) and his vehicle, as well as the house in Pakistan.
  - Because their home was owned jointly with rights of survivorship, when one owner dies their share automatically goes to the other owner. The lawyer would still need to change the ownership legally to Aisha, removing Ismail's name from the title, but the house wouldn't have to go through probate.
  - As Ismail's small RRSP designated Aisha as the beneficiary, it didn't have to go through the probate process either.
- Name and occupation of the applicant (Aisha) and relationship to the deceased

Aisha also had to sign affidavits stating she had done a complete search and found no will for Ismail and that she had informed all potential beneficiaries (in this case, her children) that she had applied for the Certificate of Appointment. It can take a few weeks for the certificate to be granted.

Estate administration tax (probate fees) would have to be paid. They are calculated based on the value of the estate. When there is no will, in some cases the administrator must post a bond with the provincial government to protect the beneficiaries' inheritances and creditors of the estate in case the estate is not administered properly – the bond acts as security for the collection, administration and accounting of the assets of the estate. When a bond isn't necessary, beneficiaries must provide signed consent forms to waive it.

Probate

Probate is the process by which the provincial government legally confirms the executor's power by granting letters probate (in Ontario, it's called a Certificate of Appointment of Estate Trustee with a Will, or in Ismail's case, without a Will). The process also confirms the validity of a single will if more than one is found or if validity is in question for any reason.

Although there is no legal requirement to go through the probate process if there is a will, because Ismail had no will Aisha needed the Certificate of Appointment to prove that she was the legal executor of Ismail's estate to such institutions as the bank – if there is no will, probate is required. In fact, financial institutions will sometimes refuse to transfer the deceased's funds without proof of probate. Probate also prevents the possibility of the executor being held personally responsible if the will is later found to be invalid for some reason. Probate also establishes a time limit within which anyone who feels they have a claim on the estate must make their claim.

To apply for probate, Aisha needed to get the appropriate form (available online). The form asks for details about the deceased, including marriage; information about the will itself; and information about the deceased's estate, including the value of all assets.

Probate fees (properly called estate administration tax) are the fees charged by the province (except Quebec) for the probate process. Each province has its own formula for calculating probate fees (a chart is provided at the end of this book outlining estate administration taxes). In Ontario, the tax is $5 per $1,000 for the first $50,000 and $15 per $1,000 after that with no maximum. Except for home mortgages, debts are not deducted from the total value of the estate.

Ismail's estate was very small because his house was jointly owned and a beneficiary was named for his RRSP. When property, such as a home, is owned jointly (that is, registered as joint tenants with right of survivorship), it passes directly to the surviving co-owner and doesn't form part of the estate, and therefore is not subject to probate.

The same applies when beneficiaries – other than the estate itself – are named on life insurance policies, annuities and RRSPs: they transfer directly to the beneficiary without becoming part of the estate, and the beneficiaries can have access to them immediately.

Distributions

Before any distributions can be made from the estate to the beneficiaries, any outstanding debts have to be paid. Final income taxes have to be paid before final distributions are made from the estate.

In the absence of a will, the rules of inheritance come into play. The rules are inflexible, so you must abide by the court's decision – the surviving family does not get to decide what happens to the deceased's property. Because Ismail was legally married and had children, his surviving spouse would get the largest share of his estate (for example, in Ontario the first $200,000), with the rest divided among the spouse and children, with one-third going to the spouse and two-thirds being divided among the six children. If Ismail had not been married or had not had children, his parents or, in the absence of parents, his siblings, would have received his assets. If no next of kin can be found, the assets of someone who dies without a will revert to the government. Note that common law spouses have inheritance rights in some provinces but not in others. When there's no will, nothing from the deceased's estate can be left to charity or to friends.

Because three of Aisha and Ismail's children were under 18, their share of the estate was held in trust by the court, and Aisha would have to apply to the court if she needed access to this money – for unusual medical expenses or higher education, for example. By law, the children's share of the estate would be fully released to them when they turned 18 – Aisha will have no control over this.

Conclusion

Once Ismail's estate was on its way to being settled, Aisha sat down with her lawyer and prepared her own will. She had learned from her experience what a huge problem it was for the survivors when someone died without a will. Not only did the deceased lose their chance to decide who would benefit from their estate (and how and when), they also lost control over who made decisions, as executor, when they were gone. She wanted to ensure that everything would pass to her children and grandchildren as she wished.

For Aisha, now a single parent, she also wanted to ensure that she could state who she wished to care for her younger children if she were to die – without a will, the court would appoint a guardian. She also stated in her will who she wanted to leave the house to. She prepared a separate will stating what she wanted done with her property outside Ontario – her properties in Pakistan. Remembering the stress of organizing Ismail's funeral, she also specified what sort of funeral she preferred for herself. When her will was complete, she felt satisfied and at peace knowing that she had spared her children a large legal bill like the one she now faced as a result of Ismail dying without a will.

Once things were settled and Aisha was feeling less stressed, she began to think about what was next for her. She had not been recalled to work at the appliance factory. She began to think she might like to start her own catering business. She had a lot of experience – and greatly enjoyed – cooking for large family gatherings with as many as 70 people, both back in Pakistan and here in Canada. She and Ismail had renovated their kitchen some years ago to help accommodate large-scale food preparation. She would need to consider selling one of her properties in Pakistan to finance the venture and would need to set up a secured line of credit, but for the first time since Ismail's death she was feeling positive and believed that, with the help of her older children, she could make it work.

Points to think about that may apply to me:

_____

_____

_____

_____

_____

_____

_____

Questions about my situation and whether something may apply to me:

_____

_____

_____

_____

Questions to ask my advisor:

_____

_____

_____

_____

Olivia

Doing Business with Relatives

Olivia, now 60, grew up in a large Italian family in downtown Toronto, one of four girls and three boys, though two of her brothers died young. Her parents had come to Canada to make a life for themselves after the Second World War. Olivia's father worked diligently running a family grocery store, personally delivering groceries to his clientele. Her mother worked long hours in the store as well. Because they were Italian, their store windows were sometimes vandalized because Italy had been allied with Germany for a time during the war; some people took exception to the family's heritage. Nonetheless, this hardworking family prospered and, over the years, Olivia's father purchased five storefronts in their neighbourhood, which he rented out and then bestowed on his children as they grew old enough to take them over and manage them.

All of the children helped out in the store as they grew up, but school and church were always high priorities – the family attended church regularly and were strong members of their predominantly Catholic community. Olivia balanced her schoolwork with long hours working in the store. She was a conscientious worker and a good student – she became the only child in her family to attend university. She was particularly strong in languages and math. Unfortunately, because of her parents' declining health, she felt she had to withdraw from school and help out once again in the family business. Her brother and sisters were getting married and getting involved in the lives of their spouses, many of them in the construction industry.

So, after successfully completing her first year at the University of Toronto, Olivia found herself back in the family business with her brother, between them carrying the load. Olivia became quite adept at sales, marketing, purchasing and stocking the store. She developed excellent people skills dealing with salespeople and clients. She also developed an understanding of the produce market. Olivia was a bright woman, a hard worker and deeply loyal to her family. She continued working long hours in the store for almost 20 years, disregarding her own needs and interests.

Olivia's husband to be, Sylvano, was born in Italy in the 1920s, the oldest of 13 children. He worked as an apprentice cheese maker in Italy until he was in his late teens. As the eldest boy in a very large family he was responsible for helping to take care of the family. Consequently, he left school and began working at an early age. Immediately after the war, he struck out on his own and emigrated to Canada, settling in southern Ontario. When he arrived in Canada, he found a job in the cheese industry and began working on a formula to make cheese by adapting an Italian recipe to accommodate Canadian ingredients. After working for many years and saving his money, he built a cheese factory of his own and enjoyed some success. Unfortunately, the factory burned to the ground and Sylvano had no insurance. Undaunted, he began again and built his new company from the ground up.

Sylvano became friendly with Olivia's father when Sylvano began selling his cheeses at the family store. He met Olivia and was immediately charmed by her kindness. He later sent a friend to Toronto to propose to her on his behalf. Although she said no, Sylvano remained determined and continued to visit. Fourteen years later, he proposed again, this time in person. And this time, Olivia said yes. At 37, it was time for her to move out of the family's shadow and begin her own new life as the wife of a successful cheese maker. Despite their 25-year age difference, Sylvano and Olivia had a loving marriage that produced two children.

Olivia moved away from her familiar role as skilled manager of a successful business and into the new role of stay-at-home wife and mother. Her caring nature meant she excelled in her new role. She also worked hard to help her husband make his business grow, putting aside her own desires, just as she had done before, to instead look after the family's personal and business needs. In addition to running his cheese business, Sylvano made his own wine and salami on the factory premises, above which the family lived. He was a physically strong man for his age and did much of the labour required at the factory. Yet he was gentle, and worked hard to grow his business so that he could better take care of his young family, whom he doted on.

After seven years of marriage, Sylvano and Olivia decided to take a trip to Italy to visit relatives and friends Sylvano had not seen for years, many of whom Olivia had never had a chance to meet. They cruised across the Atlantic and back. The children, now three and five, became fluent in Italian during their visit. They all tremendously enjoyed their time in Italy. But on the cruise home, Sylvano began to feel ill. A few months later, he was diagnosed with colon cancer and died later that summer at the age of 69.

Olivia was now a widow at 44, with two young children and a large company to manage. Although she was quite capable of running the cheese business, Sylvano's extended family, many of whom were working at the factory, had other ideas about who should be extracting profits from the company. They coerced Olivia into selling the company to them. She and her children left their apartment above the factory and moved back to Toronto, away from what now felt like an uncaring and unhealthy environment.

Sylvano's experience of not having fire insurance taught him the value of insurance, and his life insurance was a great help to Olivia when she was left on her own. Sylvano also bought life insurance policies for Olivia and their children, which paid out dividends to the children as they grew up. Sylvano had left a will, with Olivia as income beneficiary and the children as capital beneficiaries of a spousal trust: Olivia would receive income from the trust for life and the children would receive the capital, in stages as they reached certain ages. In many ways Olivia was secure financially.

Several years after her husband's death and the sale of the cheese company, Olivia again had financial dealings with family members. With one of her sisters and her brother-in-law, she became part owner of a construction company that built houses. Olivia lived in and co-owned a home with the same sister and brother-in-law and also bought into a cottage with them. She also worked in a women's and children's clothing store with two of her sisters.

But it turned out that her assets were viewed as community property. Over the next 15 years, Olivia lost many thousands of dollars, either lent to family members and never repaid or lost in various ill-conceived business arrangements that didn't work out. To her great sadness, some of her loans to family members ended up causing rifts between the borrowers: at different times, she had lent cash to two nieces. One repaid the loan on time, with interest, while the other never bothered to pay the money back. The niece who did repay found this deeply unfair and was never again friendly with her cousin who had failed to repay. Olivia felt somehow responsible for their falling out.

She eventually moved to her own home. The support and assistance she had assumed would flow from relatives simply wasn't there because her sisters and their husbands took advantage of her generosity and naivety. Olivia was a caring person with a propensity to trust her family with her money. She knew how to run a successful business but lacked the hard-hearted attitude and toughness required to bring the same approach to dealings with her relatives.

Fortunately, Olivia finally received some good advice from a lawyer – who also happened to be a relative but who could see what was happening to Olivia at the hands of her family. He advised her to withdraw from a proposed deal with one of her brothers-in-law. As a result she saved a lot of money when the venture failed. But afterward, feeling bad about this, she lent her brother-in-law money that he never repaid because he felt she owed him for pulling out of the deal. Olivia returned to the lawyer for help, but he told her that because she had never put the loan agreement in writing, it was her word against her brother-in-law's; she was unlikely to recover the funds.

This experience prompted Olivia to take a serious look at her financial situation so that she could protect her future and her children's future. The lawyer referred her to a financial planner.

Financial Situation

Overall Financial Preparedness: ★ ★ ★ ★ ☆

Olivia's Monthly Income: $3,000

Company Pension Plan: None

Canada Pension Plan: She had been contributing her entire working life

RRSPs: $100,000

Other Investments: Various loans to family members, unlikely to be repaid, and personal investments of $300,000

Testamentary Trust: $1.1 million

Bank Account: Approx. balance $6,500

Life Insurance: $100,000

House: Owned in her name; value approx. $500,000, mortgage-free

Car: Older model, paid off

Credit Cards: One, paid in full each month

Other Debts: None

Credit History: Very good

> **Will:** Olivia had a will naming her children as beneficiaries (part immediately, part when they reach age 25 if they are younger than that on her death)

Main Issues for Olivia

Olivia's difficulties stemmed from the fact that she was a generous and trusting woman who was not receiving independent financial or legal advice. She had involved herself in a number of arrangements with relatives, believing that, as family, they would help each other. She felt that family members would always have each other's best interests at heart. It was a deep shock and disappointment for her to discover that some of her relatives had only their own interests in mind, apparently not caring if she suffered as a result.

Olivia talked with the financial advisor about how she could get a better idea of when it was a good idea to get involved in financial dealings with family members – and when it wasn't. She needed to know how to arrange such deals to protect herself in the future. The advisor said that Olivia shouldn't feel she needed to become an expert in vetting loans and business arrangements. She could talk to an advisor any time such an opportunity came up, using the advisor as a sounding board and decision partner, whether the proposal was with a relative or not.

Help for Olivia

It is essential for people in vulnerable positions to get independent, professional and objective support for their financial security. Olivia had an understandable need to remain close to her family after she was widowed, but meeting that emotional need did much damage to her financial health. Olivia was vulnerable for two reasons: she was overly trusting and she had assets that were attractive to certain relatives. Widows and widowers often find themselves in a difficult situation when they reach out to others for support, but the hand they grab onto is one seeking to take rather than give.

Olivia realized she needed an independent accountant and financial planner – not related to her or any of her family members – to advise her on her financial affairs. With this newfound professional support, she would be able protect herself and her children's legacy. Olivia's financial planner and her lawyer gave her some guidelines for doing business with relatives:

- **Complete due diligence on every deal.** If it is a business venture, is there a business plan and does it make sense? Who else is supporting the venture, and to what degree? Get as much information about the venture as you can. You can even request a credit report on the relative asking for your involvement. If it's a loan, is it for a purpose you consider valid?
- **Seek expert advice.** If you are lending money, talk to an investment advisor about the loan agreement. Loans

between relatives must be treated the same way as loans between strangers. Have a legal written loan agreement. If you are partnering in a business venture, talk to a business lawyer, a business advisor and/or an accountant to make sure the partnership arrangement is fair. It's important to always seek your own counsel. Using the same lawyer, accountant or advisor as your relative could cause a conflict of interest, as well as leaving you wondering if you're getting advice that's in your interest or your relative's.

- **Get everything in writing.** You would put agreements with strangers in writing, so do the same with agreements with relatives. If you are lending money, the loan agreement needs to state the interest rate and repayment terms. Charging interest is fair. You can help your relative by charging less than a bank would, but you must still earn some interest, just as you would if you placed your money in any other investment or in a savings account. The agreement should describe what will happen if payments are missed or if responsibilities are not met.

- **Think about the whole family.** Consider whether the arrangement could negatively affect the family. Could it be seen as favouritism? Will it seem fair? Try to imagine the worst-case scenario from others' points of view.

- **Be cautious about co-signing.** If your relative wants you to co-sign a loan from another source, understand that you will be responsible for the loan if your relative defaults. Consider carefully whether you are willing to do this.

- **Consider your complete financial situation.** Talk to your accountant about whether the arrangement could have tax consequences for you. Discuss with your financial planner whether the arrangement could endanger your retirement plans. Include in the agreement what happens if either you or the relative you're dealing with dies before the loan is repaid or while the business venture is operating.
- **Learn to say no.** Sometimes, the loan or business deal just isn't a good idea. If you feel uneasy about the proposal for any reason, you must say no. Explain to your relative that the deal is not in the best interests of you or of family harmony. If the requested loan is more than you can afford, say so.

Conclusion

For Olivia, it was a hard lesson to learn that she must treat business and financial arrangements with relatives the same way she would treat agreements with strangers: she needed to complete her due diligence on every arrangement, seek professional legal and financial advice and overrule her instinct to always trust family without question. She had to learn that she must never assume that just because someone was related to her, they would treat her generously – or even fairly.

But she learned and was therefore able to protect her retirement by approaching family deals with the same business sense she had applied to decades of managing successful businesses. Gradually, her extended family began to respect her for this.

Points to think about that may apply to me:

_____

_____

_____

_____

_____

_____

_____

_____

Questions about my situation and whether something may apply to me:

_____

_____

_____

_____

Questions to ask my advisor:

_____

_____

_____

_____

Paul

Dealing with Denial of the Inevitable

Barbara was just finishing teachers college when she met Bill. He was charming and romantic and very positive and outgoing – Barbara thought he was the perfect man for her. They seemed to have a great deal in common. They were together for only eight months before they were married. Barbara was just 22.

But Barbara soon realized that "perfect" was hardly the word to describe their relationship after the wedding. Bill was charming alright, but that wasn't enough to build a successful marriage. Barbara quickly learned that Bill was something of a con man and couldn't hold down a job. He was forever coming up with schemes and was always on the brink of something big. Unfortunately, he was also always on the brink of trouble – trouble that, according to Bill, was never his fault.

Barbara wanted their marriage to work, and she tried to find the balance between encouraging his ambitions and nagging him to get a real job. But when she found out he was using his charm on several other women in the community, she'd had enough. She gave up on Bill and their marriage, moved out and filed for divorce, after just a year of marriage. Bill quickly disappeared from her life.

Barbara greatly enjoyed her job teaching elementary school and it helped her get over her experience with Bill. Her fellow teachers became her closest friends: a group of seven women teachers at Barbara's school often planned outings together. When some of them decided to join a bowling league, they talked Barbara into joining too. So one night each week, Barbara went out to socialize and have some fun at the bowling alley with her friends.

It was at the bowling alley a couple of years later that Barbara met Paul. He was in his last year of high school and worked at the bowling alley part time during the school year and full time in the summers. Barbara found herself looking for him when she came in, and he often sat with her group when he got off work, enjoying their camaraderie and occasionally bowling with them.

Paul was attracted to Barbara and her friends. They were friendly and didn't appear to find his youthfulness a problem – Barbara was seven years older than he was.

Barbara really liked Paul. He was friendly, intelligent, mature and sensitive. Chatting with him, she learned that he was entering the social work program at college, majoring in child and youth services. She felt there was something special about Paul, and over the months they became good friends. After he began his college courses, they started to see each other outside the bowling alley.

Barbara's first marriage had been a disaster, so she was hesitant to try again. But she knew Paul was nothing like Bill. He slowly persuaded her to try again, and they were married when he completed college. Paul and Barbara's age difference didn't matter to either of them. They planned to have children together.

Barbara continued to teach elementary school and Paul got a job as an educational assistant at a local high school. They were happy together and life was good. Two years later, Barbara gave birth to a healthy baby boy they named Mark. Because Barbara's income was higher than Paul's, they decided that he would stay home with the baby, even though at that time the government did not provide paid parental leave for fathers.

Paul loved looking after their baby and became a pioneer for father's rights. He talked his employer into letting him take a year off work without losing his seniority or his pension benefits. When their daughter, Janice, was born two years later, Paul again took parental leave for a year.

Both children grew up happy and healthy. Janice was a good student and was an excellent competitive swimmer.

Barbara was especially proud of her. Mark was an average student and loved to write poetry. As a family, they bowled regularly – it was their favourite way to spend time together. They were also great baseball fans and often attended games.

The years went by happily. Barbara, at 59 had retired from full-time teaching but continued to supply teach occasionally. Paul, at 52, was now a full-time child and youth worker in an elementary school. After she retired, Barbara headed to Florida for two weeks with one of her friends to watch baseball spring training. She still got together with the same group of seven teachers several times each year. They still bowled, and in the summer they met at a cottage for a weekend or at each other's homes for barbecues.

Paul and Barbara's son, Mark, at 30, was working part time driving a truck and still lived at home. He still wrote poetry and hadn't decided what to do with his life. Janice was in her third year of university, having taken a few years off after high school to travel. She swam competitively on her university team and knew where she was going in life.

Barbara had been the one who handled the family finances throughout their marriage, largely because when they got married the accounts and assets had all been hers – Paul had just finished college and had very little. Barbara met with a financial advisor regularly. Paul was comfortable leaving all the financial details to Barbara. He trusted her completely – they had always shared and divided the responsibilities of married life based on their skills and preferences.

Barbara had a small RRSP account and both she and Paul had decent pensions. Barbara had two non-registered investment accounts. The advisor recommended that the accounts be in both their names for estate planning purposes. Barbara told her advisor that she wanted one bank account just in her name because she used the money to buy special things for her daughter, whom she especially doted on. She didn't want Paul to worry about those purchases. Barbara also had an "in trust for" account for Janice along with an RESP for her. She hadn't set anything up for Mark because it appeared he wouldn't be pursuing higher education. Paul and Barbara owned their house jointly and still had a small mortgage. They also had some line of credit debt related to their daughter's university fees and residence costs.

At one meeting, the financial advisor asked whether Paul and Barbara had wills and powers of attorney. Barbara said they had both made wills years ago, but didn't have powers of attorney. Barbara said there was no need to update their wills "because nothing much had changed." She didn't think they needed powers of attorney yet – they were healthy. They would do that when they were older, she said. Her advisor urged her to update their wills and prepare powers of attorney, saying that everyone needed these documents because the unexpected can happen to anyone at any time, regardless of their age or health. Barbara changed the subject.

In the winter of the year she retired, Barbara was diagnosed with breast cancer. She had surgery and the prognosis was very good. Immediately after the surgery, the doctors told her the cancer had been discovered early, thanks to routine screening, and that they believed they had been able to remove it all. They told Barbara it was unlikely she would need chemotherapy or radiation treatment.

Three weeks later, however, when the oncologist received the biopsy results, Barbara was told that the cancer had actually been an aggressive type and that she should have both chemotherapy and radiation to make sure she was free of cancer. So during the spring, Barbara underwent both treatments. She had few side effects, and when treatment was over, she figured that was the end of that. She was fine.

But the following January, Barbara found a lump on her scalp. It seemed to be a cyst, and her family doctor agreed. Because of her history of cancer, however, the doctor recommended a biopsy. While she was waiting for the results, Barbara made her trip to Florida for baseball training camp, not in the least concerned.

Barbara came back to the news that the lump was not a cyst but melanoma, the most dangerous of skin cancers. She began treatment and remained positive – her previous cancer had been cured and she believed this one would be too. Paul was not so sure – he was deeply afraid. He wanted to talk with Barbara about what the future might hold, believing that with two children, they should make plans, just in case. But for the first time in their marriage, he found it difficult to discuss an uncomfortable subject with his wife. Whenever he tried to bring up the topic of getting things in order, she laughed it off, telling him he was worrying over nothing.

It seemed that every time Barbara saw her oncologist, her cancer had spread to a new location: elsewhere on her skin, her bones, her liver and finally her lungs. Yet she still believed she would get better and brushed off Paul's increasingly urgent attempts to discuss planning for the worst. She said there was no need to worry about that – she was taking treatment and would get better. Paul couldn't understand it. To him the probable outcome was clear.

Barbara eventually found she was losing her mobility and could get around only using a cane. In August she went on a cottage weekend with her friends, but she spent most of the weekend laying down in the main room listening to her friends talk. A week after she got home from the cottage she was admitted to the hospital and quickly fell into a coma. Barbara died less than two years after her first cancer diagnosis. She had not updated her will or written a power of attorney, and she had not discussed her complete financial situation with her husband.

After the funeral, Paul met with Barbara's financial advisor, who asked if Barbara had updated her will before she had died, as the advisor had urged her to do. Paul said he believed she hadn't. He had called the lawyer they had used in the past, but the lawyer couldn't find their wills. In fact, the lawyer denied that she had ever done wills for them – she remembered only handling their house purchase. The lawyer had moved her office twice since then and had disposed of many records. Paul searched at home and found draft wills for both him and Barbara, clearly prepared by that lawyer, but they were unsigned and therefore invalid and had been prepared over 10 years previously. Without a valid will, Barbara had died intestate.

Paul and the advisor took stock of the situation.

Financial Situation

Overall Financial Preparedness: ★ ★ ☆ ☆ ☆

Paul's Monthly Income: $5,000

Barbara's Monthly Income: Pension income, $3,000

Company Pension Plans: Both had paid into company plans their entire working lives

Canada Pension Plan: Both had paid into it their entire working lives

RRSPs: Barbara's plan valued at approx. $40,000, Paul named as beneficiary

---

Other Investments: In Trust For account for Janice in Barbara's name; non-registered account valued at $30,000 in Barbara's name; RESP for Janice, balance approx. $12,000

Bank Account: 1 joint account; 1 account in Barbara's name

Life Insurance: $50,000 on each, with the other named as beneficiary

House: Joint ownership with right of survivorship, valued at $250,000; $30,000 mortgage

Cars: 1 older model, paid off; 1 newer model, $425 monthly payment

Credit Cards: 1 joint account; paid in full each month

Other Debts: line of credit, balance approx. $23,000

Credit History: Paul had a good credit history

Wills: Neither Paul nor Barbara has a valid will, only unsigned drafts

Main Issues for Paul

Paul was the beneficiary of Barbara's RRSP, so he was able to transfer it to an RRSP for himself. The joint bank account remained accessible to him and was easily changed to an account in his name. Barbara had a small amount of life insurance, which covered the funeral costs and some other immediate expenses, so the family was not immediately in a cash crisis. But two major issues would take time to sort out:

- Barbara had died intestate, thus greatly complicating the process of settling her estate.
- Paul discovered that Barbara had four accounts in her name only: a bank account, an investment account and the RESP and "in trust for" (ITF) accounts for Janice.

The accounts that were in Barbara's name were frozen on her death, because she had no valid will, and would remain so until Paul had applied for and received a Certificate of Appointment to administer Barbara's estate and was able to provide the bank with notarized letters of indemnity. Meanwhile, money couldn't be taken from these accounts, even though they would need funds for Janice's tuition fees soon.

Help for Paul

Paul met with a lawyer to complete the court paperwork that would allow Paul to be appointed administrator of Barbara's estate. The whole process of settling the estate took over six months and cost over $6,000. Finally, after all the forms had been sent in and all the proper documents issued, the accounts could be transferred to Paul and Janice. Dying without a valid will is much more expensive, and much more trouble, than the cost and time of preparing wills and powers of attorney with a lawyer.

Paul learned the hard way why it's important to update wills every few years and to ensure that all accounts are accessible to surviving family members. If Paul and Barbara had been in the habit of updating their wills regularly, they would have discovered that the originals had been lost the first time they did an update. Paul now saw the wisdom of keeping copies of all documents safely at home and reviewing them regularly to determine whether any updates or changes are needed. He also realized he should have been more aware of the family's full financial situation. He also admitted he should have been more insistent with Barbara about planning for the inevitable.

Paul and his children made an appointment with the lawyer soon after to draw up – and sign – wills for all of them. They made a note to update them in five years. They also wrote powers of attorney so that if any of them became incapacitated, a family member would be able to make decisions for them.

Paul expressed to the lawyer his confusion and bafflement that Barbara had allowed this to happen to her family by dying without a proper will. She knew she was seriously ill, but had had enough time to update her will and get her affairs in order, but she had refused to do so. Paul just couldn't understand it – this was not the Barbara he had known for over 30 years.

The lawyer assured him it was very common for people – even if terminally ill – to avoid writing or updating their wills and otherwise preparing their finances for their own death. In fact, he said that about half of all people die without wills. The lawyer explained that many people who are sick, especially with cancer, have feelings of denial: they simply believe that they will not die of this illness. They believe they will beat it. Working through their health-care options and making decisions about their treatment also seems to keep some people from getting their affairs in order.

Others feel that if they prepare or update their will, they are admitting they might die and would therefore be giving in. It's almost as if they fear that making a will and other plans will hasten their death. They have been told to remain positive, to fight, and so they don't want to seem to be giving up, even if failing to prepare will leaves their surviving family with a financial and administrative mess – and potentially financial hardship.

Paul agreed that everyone, sick or healthy, should have their affairs in order, just in case. The lawyer said that instead of focusing on the "morbid" side of planning for death, people should think about the satisfaction they will feel if they know their surviving family will be looked after and will not face a legal and financial maze after a death – that was the most important thing.

Conclusion

Paul couldn't yet face going back to work so he took a year off. Janice took just two courses each semester in the year following her mother's death, but she didn't compete for the swim team. Her mother had been her biggest supporter, and she just didn't have the heart to compete without her. Mark continued to live at home while he looked for a full time job. He continued to write poetry, his work going in new directions after his mother's death – several of his poems were published in a literary magazine.

After his experience settling Barbara's estate, Paul made a point of spreading the message about the importance of updating wills and ensuring your finances flow smoothly after your death. When he heard someone was very ill, he made a special effort to relay his own experience, describing how Barbara had refused to update her affairs, believing until the end that there was no need, refusing to face the inevitable.

Paul went back to work after a year. He joined a bowling league and made some new friends. Janice finished her degree, a year later than planned, and Mark continued to publish his poetry. The family still bowls together.

Points to think about that may apply to me:

_____

_____

_____

_____

_____

_____

_____

_____

_____

Questions about my situation and whether something may apply to me:

_____

_____

_____

_____

_____

Questions to ask my advisor:

_____

_____

_____

_____

_____

Agatha

Losing a Partner in Business and in Life

Agatha, 57, and her husband Pablo, 56, owned a business together. They were equal partners, each providing the skills needed to make the business successful. Pablo was an electrician and did the electrical work; Agatha ran the office and business side. They had met at college – Pablo was in the electrician program and Agatha in bookkeeping. They discovered early on that they shared the dream of running their own business. They married soon after they graduated.

After a few years of gaining work experience as employees in their respective fields, they put together a business plan and launched their own electrician business. It was tough at first, with both of them putting all their effort, time and money into the business. They lived with Agatha's parents because at the beginning they weren't making any money. But after two years of hard work, dedication and sacrifice, their business began to turn a profit. They rented a tiny house and ran the business from the spare bedroom.

Pablo and Agatha wanted a family and had three children while they were still in their 20s, even though money was very tight and there was no money for extras – everything went back into the business. While the children were young, the couple hired a part-time office manager so that Agatha could look after the children herself.

The couple made a point of going out together once a week, trying to surprise each other with unexpected low-cost dates. With the children, they enjoyed the outdoors, camping and spending time with friends.

The business thrived as a result of their hard work, especially Pablo's – he never said no to an emergency call, no matter the time of day or night. As a result, Agatha and Pablo were able to save enough money to buy a house. They set up their business office and a work room for Pablo in the basement. With the help of Agatha's landscaper father, they turned the back yard into a woodland retreat, complete with a fire pit, pond and a small waterfall. The family often camped in their own back yard.

Their business continued to grow. They expanded their office to accommodate part-time help, forged relationships with subcontracting electricians to help Pablo when they were very busy and bought new equipment.

The years went by, the children grew and life continued to be good. Two of Agatha and Pablo's children went on to further education after high school: their second daughter was in college studying accounting, and their son was pursuing a degree in electrical engineering. Both children hoped to become involved in their parents' business and, when they were home during school holidays, they helped out. Their elder daughter had married and was running a business of her own, a thriving home daycare.

Agatha and Pablo didn't manage to put anything aside for retirement – they'd put all their money into the business and into helping the children with college and university. However, they had purchased small life insurance policies covering each of them many years previously.

Pablo and Agatha worked hard – maybe too hard. One spring Agatha was finally able to convince Pablo to go to the doctor for a checkup, which he hadn't done in many years. He was a little overweight, but not drastically, and he felt healthy otherwise. He enjoyed his beer but tried to watch what he ate. He agreed to have a checkup in part just so he could prove to Agatha that he was fine. But the results were not good. The doctor informed Pablo that his blood pressure was dangerously high. At the follow-up appointment, the doctor had more bad news: Pablo's blood work had shown that his cholesterol was very high, too. The doctor told him he needed to get some exercise, start medication, lose some weight and be even more careful about what he ate. Most importantly, he needed to find ways to reduce his stress.

Pablo was reluctant to make any changes. He took the medication the doctor had prescribed, but said he didn't have time to exercise and that his job was stressful by nature and there was nothing he could do about it. He continued to work very long hours. He was embarrassed about having to avoid certain foods and to cut back on the beer when he was out with his friends, so he tended to ignore the doctor's instructions. Agatha was deeply concerned.

A day came when Pablo didn't stir when Agatha got up in the morning. He'd been up late the night before so she thought nothing of it. But after she had dressed and started making breakfast, and Pablo still hadn't come downstairs, she went up to wake him. He had a service call at 8:00 and he wouldn't want to be late. When Agatha entered the bedroom, she saw that he was in exactly the same position he had been in an hour ago. She touched his shoulder and knew instantly. He was gone.

The ambulance came and took Pablo to the hospital. The children came to the house and accompanied Agatha to the hospital. There, a doctor told her that it appeared that Pablo had had a stroke and died in his sleep.

Agatha and her children helped each other through the days and weeks that followed, through the funeral and through the paperwork and documentation and organizing that follow any death. During that time, one of their subcontractor electricians covered some of Pablo's emergency calls, and Agatha and her accounting student daughter were able to cover the basics in the office.

But Agatha knew that soon she would have to decide what she was going to do with the business. And if she didn't make sure the business could keep going, she was in trouble. She had no retirement savings, Pablo's life insurance was far too small to support her for the rest of her life, and she didn't want to retire now anyway. Her children were not ready to join her in the business full time. Her son wasn't a qualified electrician yet and still had very little experience. It would be a few years before he was ready to take on the role of lead electrician.

Agatha met with a financial planner who specialized in working with self-employed people and small-business owners.

Financial Situation

Overall Financial Preparedness: ★ ★ ★ ☆ ☆

Pablo's Monthly Income: $4,500 from the business

Agatha's Monthly Income: $3,000 from the business

Company Pension Plan: None

Canada Pension Plan: Pablo and Agatha have both paid into it since they started their business approx. 30 years ago, but had never reached the maximum payment

---

RRSPs: None

Other Investments: Business partnership

Bank Account: Joint, balance approx. $7,500; plus a separate business account

Life Insurance: $90,000 on each, naming the other as beneficiary

House: Joint ownership with right of survivorship, value $475,000; mortgage of $40,000

Car: In Agatha's name, paid off; business-owned van, monthly payments $525

Credit Cards: 1 in business's name; 2 joint cards, carrying combined balance $5,250

Other Debts: None

Agatha's Credit History: Good

Will: Pablo had a will leaving all assets to Agatha and naming her as executor

Main Issues for Agatha

With Pablo's death, Agatha became the sole owner of the business. So, in addition to her personal finances and future, she also needed to consider the future of the business. The two were, of course, tightly linked. The advisor clarified the situation as follows:

- Agatha needed to have her business evaluated to determine its worth. She must decide whether to sell the business or to hire one or more electricians to work for her. If she kept the business, she would have to determine if, and when, to make any new electricians partners, or whether she would continue as the sole owner of the business and have the electricians work as her employees.

- Agatha needed to increase the amount of life insurance she had – the $90,000 policy she and Pablo had purchased many years ago was not sufficient. Two of her children were still dependent on her and incurring expenses in post-secondary education. Her other daughter was saving to buy a house with her husband. Agatha wanted to make sure her children were provided for if she were to die.

- Agatha needed to consider her retirement.

Help for Agatha

Agatha needed to see a lawyer to discuss the structure of her company. Because her business partner had died, the partnership automatically dissolved. She needed to decide whether to form another partnership with a new business partner or to be a sole proprietor or to incorporate.

Life Insurance

Agatha discussed life insurance with her financial advisor. To increase her current coverage, she would need to go through the life insurance underwriting process. She would have to answer medical questions about her own and her family's health history and she would be required to take basic tests. Because she was healthy, it made sense to get more coverage now. If she waited until she was older or had a health problem, the insurance company could decline coverage.

If it didn't decline coverage, it would certainly charge a much higher premium on the policy – that is, they would "rate" the policy. For example, everyone starts with a rating of 100% (this is the probability that someone will die at some point). If a person is rated on a policy because of health issues, the insurance company believes that the probability of that person dying is much higher. Policies can be rated anywhere from 150% to 300%. If a monthly policy premium is regularly $100 and the person is rated at 150%, then the premium will be $150.

In situations where the surviving spouse wants to have coverage in place to ensure the financial stability of their children if something happened, and if this is the only option of providing for the children if their parent died, it is sometimes possible to get the insurance company to rate a policy rather than declining it. In situations where coverage is really needed, insurance companies do want to help and provide that coverage, but they will charge for the additional risk they are taking on.

Agatha needed enough insurance to provide for her three children's needs. She also wanted to provide enough for the two children interested in taking over the business to buy out their older sister, who had no interest in the business but had an equal right to Agatha's estate. Agatha would leave her assets, including her share of the business, to her three children. The three children would also be beneficiaries of the life insurance policy. If Agatha were to get a new business partner, the insurance money could also be used to purchase Agatha's new partner's share of the business. Without this coverage, the children could lose their chance to be part of the business their parents had founded.

Retirement Planning

Although Agatha knew she wasn't ready to retire, thinking about what to do with her business had got her thinking about the day when she would retire. Not only was she not ready to retire, she also had not done any retirement planning. She and Pablo had always put all their surplus cash back into the business – they had no savings and of course no company pension.

Agatha and her financial advisor decided that Agatha would begin her retirement savings with the money from Pablo's life insurance policy. She would contribute the insurance proceeds to a TFSA and to her RRSP, maximizing both contributions. They looked at what her expenses would be in retirement, and figured out how much she would need to save to ensure she had enough to cover those expenses, factoring in the amount of CPP she could expect to receive from her plan and Pablo's. Agatha said she would be comfortable working for another 10 years, so she had those years during which she could save, but she would need a fairly aggressive investment plan for the first half of that time.

Conclusion

After subcontracting work to several electricians, Agatha found one who was especially conscientious, hard-working and well-liked by their customers – and he was interested in becoming a partner in Agatha's business. Together with a lawyer and Agatha's children, they worked out a partnership agreement that included a provision to allow Agatha's junior electrician son and accountant daughter to join the business when they were ready.

Agatha was able to hand over the labour side of the business to her new partner and, increasingly, her son, while she concentrated on looking after her side of things, and together they were able to grow the business into markets they hadn't reached before. Over time, her children took on larger roles in their parents' business.

Points to think about that may apply to me:

_____

_____

_____

_____

_____

_____

_____

_____

_____

Questions about my situation and whether something may apply to me:

_____

_____

_____

_____

Questions to ask my advisor:

_____

_____

_____

_____

_____

Kathleen and Andrew

Getting Your Affairs in Order

Kathleen and Andrew, now in their 70s, had immigrated from the United Kingdom in the early 1960s. They had met in the 50s, while Britain was rebuilding after the war. They had come from very different backgrounds: Andrew had been a home child and grew up in an orphanage after his parents died in the Blitz. Kathleen was from a well-established country family. She was confident, well-educated and accomplished. She was in her late teens, working for a local newspaper, when she met Andrew. He was working in construction in the city but longed to get out into the clean air. He was ambitious and had learned to look after himself. The day he left the orphanage, he promised himself his children would never have to live like that. Growing up without a family, he was determined to build one of his own.

The pair met at a riding stable. Andrew had taken the bus there on his day off, hoping to trade some labour for a chance to learn to ride – horses fascinated him. Kathleen was there with her friend, whose parents owned the stable. The two girls, riders since toddlerhood, had delighted in taking on the challenge of teaching a good-looking city boy to ride. They spent that day together, and many more like it. Even though he had grown up in the city, Andrew loved horses and had a feel for them. Soon, Kathleen and Andrew were together whenever he had time off work.

Andrew believed more opportunity for him lay outside Britain. It wasn't hard to convince the adventurous Kathleen that they could build a happy life in Canada. They married and left for Canada shortly thereafter. Andrew found work as a maintenance and renovation supervisor for a school board in a small city, and Kathleen found a part-time job with a community newspaper. They rented a house on the outskirts of the city, finding time to visit a nearby riding stable when they could. Soon, they welcomed the first of their six children.

Two more children were born in the next five years. Soon after, the couple took on the job of managing a small horse farm, while Andrew continued in his role at the school board. The farm job included the use of the smaller of two homes on the property. The family revelled in their new country life. The children could learn to ride and have plenty of fresh air and sunshine. Andrew was always building – a shed, an addition to the house, a new barn. They were happy. Three more children came in quick succession.

When the owner of the property decided to sell, he gave Andrew and Kathleen right of first refusal, and they quickly agreed they would buy it. With their savings, help from Kathleen's parents and a mortgage, the farm was theirs. They moved into the larger house and grew the farm into a modest part-time business, boarding horses and offering trail rides on the weekend.

Over the years, two of Kathleen's brothers, as well as her widowed mother, had also immigrated to the area. There was always a family gathering happening at the farm. There were lots of cousins for the kids to play with and great camaraderie and plenty of healthy competition. The extended family remained close as the children grew into adulthood and began to have families of their own. It was a big part of their lives for the family to gather together as often as possible. Andrew's dream of a big, loving family had come true.

Much as they loved their home, after Andrew retired from the school board, he and Kathleen began to travel. As their children moved away, it seemed natural to take trips to see them and their expanding brood of grandchildren.

One year, the family held a big 50th wedding anniversary party for Kathleen and Andrew. Friends and family surrounded them with love and good wishes. This was a couple that were role models for everyone, more in love now than when they married. They knew how to enjoy life, to appreciate the outdoors and to work hard, but they also knew when to take time to relax and spend time with those they loved.

Shortly after the party, Andrew complained of chest pains. He went to the doctor and after several tests found out he had some problems with his heart. The doctor prescribed medication that would help, but said the problem was likely to recur.

The news made the couple recognize that at some time in the not too distant future, one of them would leave the other. It was something neither wanted to think about, but they realized that they had to talk about it. Talking about death isn't easy, and when it's possibly your own death you're discussing, it's even harder. Andrew and Kathleen thought it would be a good idea to bring in a third party, so they met with their financial advisor, who took stock of their situation and made some recommendations.

Financial Situation

Overall Financial Preparedness: ★ ★ ☆ ☆ ☆

Andrew's Monthly Income: CPP $1,000, company pension, $2000

Kathleen's Monthly Income: Approx. $1,000 (from farm activities), CPP $200

Company Pension Plan: Andrew paid into it for 38 years; Kathleen has none

Canada Pension Plan: Andrew paid into it for 38 years; Kathleen for 17 years (part time)

RRSPs: RRSPs have been converted to Registered Retirement Income Funds paying $1,500 quarterly; each names the other as successor annuitants

Other Investments: None

Bank Account: 1 joint account; 1 account in Andrew's name; 1 in Kathleen's name; combined approx. balance $8,400

Life Insurance: $100,000 on Andrew from prior employer; no beneficiary named; none on Kathleen

House/Farm: Owned in Andrew's name, valued at $1.5 million; mortgage-free

Vehicles: 2 older cars, paid off; tractor, paid off

Credit Cards: 1 joint card, paid off monthly

Other Debts: None

Credit History: Andrew's is good; Kathleen's limited to one credit card

Wills: None

Main Issues for Kathleen and Andrew

As they talked with their financial advisor, Kathleen and Andrew quickly realized that getting things in order was one of the smartest things they could do. The advisor went over all the financial details, potential complications and paperwork surrounding a death.

Estate planning is all about personal choice – it is not the same for everyone. There are many different routes you can take. One reason to work with a professional is to determine what will work best for you and your family. With the guidance of their advisor, Kathleen and Andrew were able to think logically about how one of them would live when the other died, and about their children and grandchildren and what they wanted to leave them. Getting all the information in advance helped them consider and look after the final requirements.

The surviving spouse would still need to grieve and take the time to deal with their loss, but they wouldn't have to worry about as much of the paperwork that comes with the death of a spouse, and they wouldn't be thrown into financial turmoil – there would be no surprises. Another benefit of having everything planned out is that the estate can be settled promptly, so beneficiaries' needs are looked after quickly.

Help for Kathleen and Andrew

During their planning session, Andrew and Kathleen identified with their planner the major issues they needed to deal with.

- Life insurance
- Joint ownership of assets (bank accounts, farm)
- Government assistance for surviving spouse
- Funeral planning and prepayment
- Trust funds for their grandchildren
- Wills

Life Insurance

Some of these issues, even though very important, could be dealt with quickly and easily. On checking Andrew's company life insurance policy, they found that a beneficiary had never been named. Andrew simply contacted the benefits administrator for the school board and asked them to change the beneficiary on his policy from his estate to Kathleen. Their advisor noted in their financial plan that if Kathleen predeceased Andrew, he would need to change the beneficiary again.

Kathleen did not have life insurance. Because of the uncertainty of the situation, their financial planner recommended that they not purchase any for her at that time.

Joint Ownership of Assets

Changing the ownership of the bank accounts was a simple matter of visiting their branch and having the accounts paperwork changed so that they were all joint accounts. The advantage of this is that on the death of one spouse, the accounts automatically pass to the other without becoming part of the estate (and thus avoiding probate fees). More importantly, the accounts would not be frozen on the account holder's death, as accounts held only by the deceased would be, meaning the surviving spouse would have uninterrupted access to the account.

To change the ownership of the house and farm property from only Andrew to both of them, the couple met with their lawyer to have the land title transferred. In addition to the lawyer's fee, the transfer involved a registration fee of approximately $500.

Government Assistance

The financial planner told the couple about the various types of government assistance that were available to surviving spouses: death benefit, allowance for survivors and survivor's benefits. Together they figured out which they would qualify for and noted what documents they would need when they applied and where they could get the current forms when the time came. Because forms change from time to time, making a note of where to get them when the time comes is better than printing the forms now and keeping them on hand.

Funeral Planning and Prepayment

Next, the financial planner brought up the subject of funerals. This is not an easy topic to discuss, but making decisions when there's no time pressure and everyone is feeling fine is much easier than doing it when a surviving spouse is stressed and grieving and the matter is urgent. Andrew and Kathleen assured their advisor they would discuss the matter with their children and prepare funeral plans and that they would then prepay for the arrangements. The advisor noted this in their plan so that everyone would know a funeral had already been planned and paid for.

There are options available for prepaying for a funeral: you can pay the full amount up front, pay a certain amount each year for a number of years or make monthly payments. Because Andrew knows he has some health problems, he needed to talk to the funeral home about whether he would be able to make payments over time or if he would have to pay it all up front. Even if he was able to make the payments over time he may still not be eligible for insurance coverage for any amount outstanding at his death. This means that if Andrew died before he had paid the full amount, the remaining balance would be due at the time of the funeral.

Making Wills and Creating a Trust Fund

Finally, Andrew and Kathleen made wills, which they had never gotten around to doing before. Because they both wanted the other to be able to continue to live in their current home, they each left all their assets to the other. They also named the other as executor, selecting two of their children as the backup executors.

The couple wanted, when they were both gone, for their children and grandchildren to benefit from their estate, so they created a draft plan that the surviving spouse would formalize as part of his or her updated will after the first spouse died. In the update, they would leave assets to each of their six children and set up a testamentary trust for their 10 grandchildren.

With a trust, the grandchildren would receive legacies from their grandparents without having to wait for their own parents to pass away, but the money would be protected until each grandchild was mature enough to manage it. Kathleen and Andrew chose for the grandchildren to receive their legacies in steps, when they turned 18 and 24. Part of the assets would pass to them at age 18 to help them pay for further education (tuition and living expenses while at school) or to purchase a car. The rest of the money would pass to them at age 24 to help them get started with their own lives. They could use the money at their own discretion – for example, for a down payment on a house, for travel or for anything else they needed to get them started in life.

The surviving spouse would need to update their will after the other dies.

The financial planner recorded their decisions on all these matters, organized all the paperwork and left the couple with a roadmap ready for whoever would need it.

Conclusion

Andrew remained reasonably healthy for several more years, with just a few recurrences of his heart condition, but there came a day when he really didn't feel well. He had bad chest pains and shortness of breath. As Kathleen packed a bag for him, Andrew stood holding the pasture fence, looking at his beloved horses for what he thought could be the last time.

Kathleen drove him to the hospital, he was admitted and all of the children were called and advised that it didn't look good. Within 24 hours children and grandchildren had gathered at the hospital, preparing to say goodbye. It was time, and while it wasn't easy, everyone was able to give a final hug to a cherished husband, father and grandfather.

When Andrew passed away, Kathleen was surrounded by her family, who helped her tremendously, but it was as if half of her was gone. She felt she couldn't do anything. She was relieved that the final financial planning they had done meant she didn't need to tend to those matters now. She would not have been able to face them. All she could do was grieve. She did the few things she had to do, such as visiting the lawyer to update her will according to the plan they had made and signing the government benefit application forms her daughter prepared for her.

As the initial shock subsided over the months, Kathleen began to feel restless. She decided to take a long trip to visit each of her children in turn, family now more important to her than ever. She entrusted her horses and her home to her nephew and spent the next year travelling, staying with each of her grown children in turn, enjoying her grandchildren and telling stories of all the happy times she and Andrew had had.

Points to think about that may apply to me:

_____

_____

_____

_____

_____

_____

_____

_____

Questions about my situation and whether something may apply to me:

_____

_____

_____

_____

Questions to ask my advisor:

_____

_____

_____

_____

Additional
Resources

For additional questions or to discuss your specific situation, contact us today to schedule your free 30-minute call.

Dedicated Financial Solutions
714 Burnhamthorpe Rd. E.,
Mississauga, ON Canada L4Y 2X3

Telephone: 905-896-8373
Toll free: 1-866-552-9333

info@dedicatedfinancialsolutions.ca

To book Janet and Jennifer for a speaking engagement, contact info@dedicatedfinancialsolutions.ca or go to www.createwealthnow.ca/speaking.

To order additional copies of this book go to www.managingalone.ca or
use the order forms at the back of this book.

Who to Contact After Your Spouse Has Died

When your spouse dies, you will need to contact some or all of the following people and organizations as soon as possible:

- Your closest family and friends – ask them to contact other friends and relatives for you
- Your spouse's employer, and former employers, about pensions and any pay that might be due to your spouse, if he or she was working
- Insurance companies about any life policies on your spouse; update policies for which the deceased was a beneficiary (such as your own) and change or cancel supplemental health insurance
- Canada Pension (or Quebec Pension) and Veterans' Affairs to claim death benefits and survivors benefits
- Service Canada to cancel payments under all income security programs (Old Age Security, Veterans' Affairs benefits, Canada Pension Plan benefits or the child tax benefit)
- The provincial government to stop payments the deceased may have been receiving (such as welfare, drug benefits or disability support) and to transfer ownership of a vehicle
- A financial advisor and a lawyer to help you make decisions, complete necessary paperwork and plan for your future

- Your spouse's bank, investment firm and credit card companies to cancel, transfer or change account information – don't forget to ask the bank if the deceased had a safe deposit box
- The appropriate government offices concerning your spouse's identification cards – social insurance, health card, passport, etc.
- The municipality to transfer ownership of property
- Vehicle and home insurance companies to transfer policies to your name
- Utility companies such as telephone, cable, electricity, gas, etc. to change account information
- Your spouse's cell phone provider to cancel the service
- Your spouse's doctors if they do not already know

When you have time, or when the time comes, contact the following:

- An accountant for assistance with filing your spouse's final tax return
- Your spouse's other health care providers, such as the dentist, optometrist and chiropractor
- Newspapers and magazines to which the deceased subscribed to change subscription information or cancel
- Clubs, professional associations, alumni association and volunteer organizations
- Elections Canada to have the deceased removed from the voters list

- Online communities your spouse was part of to close accounts, such as Linked In, Facebook, Twitter and discussion forums

Make sure you also do the following:

- Obtain several original copies of the death certificate from the funeral home
- Update your own will and power of attorney

Who to Ask

It can sometimes be difficult to figure out which advisor or service provider to ask about a concern you may have. We've listed some common topics that surviving spouses may have questions about, along with where to go for help.

Ask your financial planner questions about...

- Minimizing taxes on your spouse's estate and for yourself in the future
- Transferring your spouse's assets to you
- Financial considerations if selling your house
- Establishing your own credit history
- Getting your financial affairs in order
- Investing
- Retirement planning

Ask your insurance agent questions about...

- How much insurance coverage you need and what type is best suited to your situation
- Changes to your coverage that might be needed now that your spouse is gone

Ask your lawyer questions about...

- Executors' duties
- Probate
- Writing or updating your will and power of attorney
- Setting up a trust

Ask your accountant questions about...

- Your or your spouse's tax returns
- Government benefits for surviving spouses and children
- Business finances

Estate Administration Taxes (Probate Fees)
Probate is a provincial matter, so fees vary across Canada.
Below is a summary of the costs as of 2013.

Alberta	$0 to $10,000	$25
	$10,001 to $25,000	$100
	$25,001 to $125,000	$200
	$125,001 to $250,000	$300
	$250,001 & over	$400
British Columbia	$0 to $25,000	No Fee
	$25,001 to $50,000	$208 + $6 per $1,000 over $25,000
	$50,001 & over	$358 + $14 per $1,000 over $50,000
Manitoba	$0 to $10,000	$70
	$10,001 & over	$70 + $7 per $1,000 over $10,000
New Brunswick	$0 to $5,000	$25
	$5,001 to $10,000	$50
	$10,001 to $15,000	$75
	$15,001 to $20,000	$100
	$20,001 & over	$5 per $1,000
Newfoundland & Labrador	$0 to $1,000	$60
	$1,001 & over	$60 + $5 per $1,000 over $1,000
Northwest Territories	$0 to $10,000	$25
	$10,001 to $25,000	$100
	$25,001 to $125,000	$200
	$125,001 to $250,000	$300
	$250,001 & over	$400
Nova Scotia	$0 to $10,000	$78.54
	$10,001 to $25,000	$197.48
	$25,001 to $50,000	$328.65
	$50,001 to $100,000	$920.07
	$100,001 & over	$920.07 + $15.53 per $1,000 over $100,000
Nunavut	$0 to $10,000	$25
	$10,001 to $25,000	$100
	$25,001 to $125,000	$200
	$125,001 to $250,000	$300
	$250,001 & over	$400
Ontario	$1,000 or less	No fee
	$1,001 to $50,000	$5 per $1,000
	$50,001 & over	$250 + $15 per $1,000 over $50,000
Prince Edward Island	$0 to $10,000	$50
	$10,001 to $25,000	$100
	$25,001 to $50,000	$200
	$50,001 to $100,000	$400
	$100,001 & over	$400 + $4 per $1,000 over $100,000
Quebec	Court fee for probate of a will	$102
Saskatchewan	All estates	$7 per $1,000
Yukon	$0 to $25,000	$0
	$25,001 & over	$140

More Resources

Books

Mary Francis. *The Sisterhood of Widows: Sixteen True Stories of Grief, Anger and Healing.* Morgan James, 2011.

Thomas William Deans. *Willing Wisdom: 7 Questions to Ask Before You Die.* Détente Financial Press, 2013.

Jane Blaufus. *With the [Stroke] of a Pen, Claim Your Life.* Blaufus Group, 2011.

Benjamin McLean. *The Canadian Widow's Guide to Enjoying Your Retirement Dollars and Making Them Last.* McGraw-Hill Ryerson Trade, 2001.

Maryanne Pope. *Widow's Awakening.* Pink Gazelle Productions, 2008.

Enid Stronach. *Soldier On – Overcoming Grief by Living Through It.* TRI, 2011.

Websites

Information and discussion forum for widows and widowers: www.widowed.ca

Federal Government
- Service Canada: Following a Death:
  http://www.servicecanada.gc.ca/eng/lifeevents/loss.shtml
- "Preparing Returns for Deceased Persons":
  http://www.cra-arc.gc.ca/E/pub/tg/t4011/t4011-e.html
- "What to Do Following a Death": http://www.cra-arc.gc.ca/E/pub/tg/rc4111/README.html
- Federal benefits:
  http://www.servicecanada.gc.ca/eng/lifeevents/death/survivordeathbenefits.shtml

Provincial Offices

British Columbia: "Dealing with Death":
http://www.servicebc.gov.bc.ca/life_events/death/index.html

Alberta: "Dealing with Death":
http://www.programs.alberta.ca/Living/5959.aspx?Ns=5251&N=770

Saskatchewan: "Dealing with Death":
http://www.gov.sk.ca/life-events/death/

Manitoba: "Dealing with Death":
http://residents.gov.mb.ca/death.html

Ontario: "What to Do When Someone Dies":
http://www.ontario.ca/government/what-do-when-someone-dies
Attorney General of Ontario: Estates –
Frequently Asked Questions:
http://www.attorneygeneral.jus.gov.on.ca/english/estates/estates-FAQ.asp
Law Society of Upper Canada:
- Though this information is intended for lawyers, the practice area resources provide information on topics such as how to prepare an Application for a Certificate of Appointment of Estate Trustee with a Will (or without a Will) and how to administer an estate without a will:
http://www.lsuc.on.ca/For-Lawyers/Manage-Your-Practice/Practice-Area/Lawyer-Practice-Area-Resources/

Quebec: "What to Do in the Event of Death":
http://www4.gouv.qc.ca/EN/Portail/Citoyens/Evenements/deces/Pages/accueil.aspx

New Brunswick: Death Certificate application:
https://www.pxw1.snb.ca/snb9000/product.aspx?ProductID=A001PSN6000B

Nova Scotia: "What to Do When Someone Dies":
http://www.gov.ns.ca/snsmr/life-events/what-to-do-when-someone-dies.asp

Prince Edward Island: "Death, Dying and Bereavement":
http://www.gov.pe.ca/infopei/index.php3?number=3270&lang=E

Newfoundland & Labrador: Death Certificate application:
http://www.servicenl.gov.nl.ca/birth/death_certificate/index.html

Yukon: Death:
http://www.gov.yk.ca/services/life_death.html

Northwest Territories: Vital Statistics:
http://www.hss.gov.nt.ca/vital-statistics

Nunavut: Death Certificates:
http://www.hss.gov.nu.ca/en/Vital%20Statistics%20Death.aspx

Bereavement Organizations

British Columbia Bereavement Helpline:
http://www.bcbereavementhelpline.com/

Bereaved Families of Ontario:
http://www.bereavedfamilies.net/index.htm

Grief Nova Scotia: http://griefns.com/?p=217

Military Families: Strength Behind the Uniform Shoulder to Shoulder:
http://www.familyforce.ca/sites/ShouldertoShoulder/EN/Pages/default.aspx

Managing Alone

Help someone through one of the most difficult times in life by giving them a copy of *Managing Alone*.

Please send me ___ copies of *Managing Alone* at $19.95 CDN each, shipping included. I have enclosed a cheque payable to Dedicated Financial Solutions in the amount of $_____.

Information for shipping

Full Name: _____

Mailing Address: _____

City: _____

State/Province: _____ Zip/Postal Code: _____

Email: _____

Phone: _____

Mail completed order form and cheque to:
Dedicated Financial Solutions
714 Burnhamthorpe Rd. East,
Mississauga, ON Canada L4Y 2X3

Or charge to my credit card:

Credit card type:
Visa: ❑   MasterCard: ❑   Expiry Date: _____
Card #: _____
Name on card: _____
Signature: _____

Books ship the same day that orders are received and typically arrive within 4 to 5 business days.

Managing Alone

Help someone through one of the most difficult times in life by giving them a copy of *Managing Alone*.

Please send me ___ copies of *Managing Alone* at $19.95 CDN each, shipping included. I have enclosed a cheque payable to Dedicated Financial Solutions in the amount of $_____.

Information for shipping

Full Name: _____

Mailing Address: _____

City: _____

State/Province: _____ Zip/Postal Code: _____

Email: _____

Phone: _____

Mail completed order form and cheque to:
Dedicated Financial Solutions
714 Burnhamthorpe Rd. East,
Mississauga, ON Canada L4Y 2X3

Or charge to my credit card:

Credit card type:
Visa: ❑   MasterCard: ❑   Expiry Date: _____

Card #: _____

Name on card: _____

Signature: _____

Books ship the same day that orders are received and typically arrive within 4 to 5 business days.